GOD'S
PLAN
FOR
ISRAEL

GOD'S PLAN FOR ISRAEL

A STUDY OF ROMANS 9-11

STEVEN A. KRELOFF

LOIZEAUX
Neptune, New Jersey

Library of Congress Cataloging-in-Publication Data

Kreloff, Steven A., 1952–
God's plan for Israel: a study of Romans 9-11 / Steven A. Kreloff.
Includes bibliographical references and index.
ISBN 0-87213-468-7 (pbk.)
1. Bible. N.T. Romans IX-XI—Commentaries.
2. Israel (Christian theology)—Biblical teaching. I. Title.
BS2665.3.K74   1995
227'.106—dc20   95-16044

Printed in the United States of America
10 9 8 7 6 5 4 3 2 1

In loving memory of my mother,
Florence Kreloff,
who came to believe in the Messiah of Israel
hours before entering His presence.

CONTENTS

FOREWORD

In a day when there is a drift from traditional dispensationalism toward covenant theology, Steven Kreloff's book *God's Plan for Israel* appears as a breath of fresh air. His lucid treatment of Romans 9–11 is an excellent exposition of Israel's past, present, and future.

Unlike neo-dispensationalists, who claim to be "progressive," Kreloff follows the Scripture in showing clearly the complete distinction between Israel and the church. The promises to Israel are not fulfilled in the church.

I was granted the privilege of reading the original manuscript of this book and I am delighted to endorse it. There is much need for this treatise because its subject is much misunderstood. Students and teachers of God's Word who read this book will be richly rewarded.

LEHMAN STRAUSS

PREFACE

T he title of this book states that its subject matter is God's plan for Israel. However that's only part of the story. More specifically this book is about the righteousness of God in His dealings with the Jewish people. While books abound concerning Israel and prophecy, authors seldom write about God's faithfulness in relation to the children of Jacob. Therefore I have endeavored to present an exposition of Paul's teaching in Romans 9–11 regarding the integrity of God in His dealings with Israel. I see chapters 9–11 as critical, not parenthetical, to the apostle's argument in Romans. Just as the gospel of Christ reveals the righteousness of God (Romans 1:17), God's past, present, and future dealings with Israel also demonstrate His righteous character.

The doctrines of God's sovereignty and human responsibility coexist without conflict in Romans 9–11. There is a great need among evangelicals to understand that God's sovereignty in election does not negate human responsibility in salvation or evangelism. My desire is that the readers of my commentary will not try to reconcile these two theological truths, but will conclude with Paul, "O the depth of the riches both of the wisdom and knowledge of God!" (Romans 11:33)

This exposition of Romans 9–11 originally appeared as articles in *Israel My Glory* magazine from October 1987 through January 1990. The many responses I received from readers encouraged me to present my ideas in book form.

I am immensely grateful to my friend Jackie DiNardo for her editorial work, typing, and encouragement. Without her this book would never have been a reality. Special thanks are also due to the elders and congregation of Lakeside Community Chapel for giving me the freedom to study and teach the Word of God. I am particularly grateful to the leaders of the Friends of Israel Gospel Ministry who first allowed me to put this teaching on Romans 9–11 in printed form; to my secretary Ruth McAllester, who did a variety of work associated with the commentary; to my colleague J. Michael Dyck, who took the time to proofread the text; to Paul Enns and Phil Johnson, who shared their expertise; to Dr. Lehman Strauss, who expressed confidence in the work; and to my wife Michele and our three children—Ben, Sarah, and Rachel—who persevered with me through the process of bringing this book to life.

STEVEN A. KRELOFF

INTRODUCTION

When as a university freshman I accepted Christ as my Savior, I wondered if I were the only Jewish person who had ever made this decision. In due course, while reading the New Testament I discovered that the first-century church was almost exclusively Jewish. Its members were Jewish. Its faith was in the Jewish Messiah. It believed a message that was preached in the Jewish land. It looked to the Old Testament Scriptures for spiritual understanding of New Testament truth.

In the early days of the church Jewish people were very responsive to the message of Jesus Christ. On the day of Pentecost when the church was born, three thousand Jews were saved (Acts 2:41). Soon thousands more received Christ (Acts 4:4). It seemed that before long the entire nation of Israel would repent and believe the gospel. But corrupt leadership opposed the gospel and the tide turned. Stephen, a great man of faith, was martyred and a severe persecution arose. Believers scattered across the Roman empire (Acts 8) and suddenly Jewish people were no longer being swept into God's kingdom in large numbers. Instead many Jews became bitter opponents of Christianity while multitudes of Gentiles turned to Christ for salvation.

This strange turn of events puzzled first-century Jewish

Christians. They knew the Old Testament Scriptures taught that with the coming of the Messiah, Israel would be saved and blessed and many wonderful promises would be fulfilled. However, Jesus the Messiah had come and Israel as a nation had rejected Him. The early Christians wondered what would happen to the promises God had given to Israel. Would God go back on His word? Would Israel be cast aside in favor of a largely Gentile church? These were logical questions being raised by Jewish Christians everywhere and especially at Rome.

Paul had these questions in mind when he wrote his Epistle to the Romans. In his letter he fully explained the gospel of Jesus Christ and its implications. Paul focused on the righteousness of God. In the first three chapters he put Gentiles and Jews on trial and proved that both are guilty before a holy God and in need of divine righteousness. In the next few chapters he presented Jesus Christ as the only provision of God's righteousness. Through faith in Jesus Christ a person is legally declared righteous and therefore is the recipient of a present peace and a future glory (Romans 5:1-5).

In Romans 8 Paul enlarged upon the concept of future glory by teaching that salvation in Christ Jesus is complete and will take us all the way to Heaven. He began the chapter by stating that "there is therefore now no condemnation to them which are in Christ Jesus" (8:1) and he closed the chapter by declaring that nothing "shall be able to separate us from the love of God, which is in Christ Jesus our Lord" (8:39). All the verses in between these two magnificent statements were designed to give assurance that believers are safe and secure in Christ.

Jewish believers in Rome, listening to Paul's words of security for Christ's church, questioned the validity of his assurances because they had doubts about Israel's spiritual security. As Hebrew Christians looked around their assembly and saw a predominantly Gentile church (Romans 11:13), they wondered if God was through with Israel and was replacing her with the church. If He was, they reasoned, He had not kept His Old Testament promises to Israel. If God had been unfaithful in His dealings with Israel, He could not be counted on to be faithful in His dealings with the church. Paul knew that many were doubting the integrity of God, so in Romans 9–11 he presented truths that vindicate God of any wrongdoing against His chosen nation and substantiate the righteousness of God.

The message of Romans 9–11 is not a side issue. It is not a parenthesis in Paul's letter. Instead it is central to his argument, for if God has permanently cast away Israel, His promise of security for the church means nothing. If God has treated Israel unrighteously, how can the righteousness of God be revealed in the gospel (Romans 1:16-17)? Before Paul could call the church to demonstrate a righteous lifestyle (Romans 12–16), he had to establish the fact that God is not guilty of any unrighteousness in connection with Israel.

The following commentary on Romans 9–11 shows how Paul defended the righteousness of God in His dealings with Israel and praised His mercy toward both Jews and Gentiles. The apostle revealed the means by which God has spared the Hebrew nation in the past, the reason He continues to preserve the Jewish people in the present, and the plan He has for restoring Israel to the place of privilege in the future.

Part One

ISRAEL: THE PAST

Chapter 1

PAUL'S PASSION FOR ISRAEL

Romans 9:1-5

Paul was considered a traitor to the Jewish people. He was looked upon as the Judas of Judaism. Once Israel's greatest champion for Judaism (Acts 8–9), Paul became a believer in Jesus the Messiah (Acts 9:4-6), an apostle to the Gentiles (Romans 11:13), and a teacher of salvation by grace (Romans 4). From the perspective of the Jewish people, Paul was an enemy. How wrong they were. Paul loved his people with the deepest of passions.

PAUL'S PASSION - ROMANS 9:1-3

Paul was about to address Israel's unbelief and rejection of the Messiah, and he didn't want to be misunderstood. He didn't want anyone saying, "I told you so. Paul hates us. Look how he delights in our spiritual dilemma." So before he even mentioned the shame, failure, and unbelief of Israel, he affirmed his love for his kinsmen. He wrote, "I say the truth in Christ, I lie not, my conscience also bearing me witness in the Holy Ghost, That I have great heaviness and continual sorrow in my heart" (9:1-2). Paul wanted every Jewish person to be assured that he was grief-stricken over the spiritual condition of Israel. His conscience and the Holy Spirit confirmed the genuineness of his anguish. Paul's heart was breaking for the nation of Israel.

It isn't uncommon to hear godly Christians refer to their love for the Jewish people. Paul's love, though, was so intense and so earnest that he was willing to go to Hell for eternity if it would result in the salvation of the Jewish people. He wrote, "For I could wish that myself were accursed from Christ for my brethren, my kinsmen according to the flesh" (9:3). The term "accursed" is a translation of the Greek word *anathema,* meaning "to hand someone over to God for judgment." The same thought is conveyed by the word "damnation." Paul's love for his people consumed him to the degree that, if it were possible, he was willing to be damned to Hell if they could be saved in his place.

Paul knew that he could not be damned to Hell. He had just taught the truth that nothing "shall be able to separate us from the love of God, which is in Christ Jesus our Lord" (8:39). Paul also knew that Israel could never be saved by his being lost. His words were the language of passion—not logic. He was communicating the great yearning he had for his kinsmen's salvation, a yearning so deep that he was willing to be lost forever, if that were possible.

Just because Paul's desire could not become a reality, we should not take his words lightly. Even though the apostle knew his yearning was a theological impossibility, he still meant what he said and he called upon Christ, his conscience, and the Holy Spirit to verify the depth of his love for Israel (9:1-2).

Very few believers can relate to this depth of love. There may be people for whom we would be willing to die, but would we be willing to spend eternity in Hell for them? Paul's love dominated his missionary zeal. His heart broke over Israel's failure to embrace Christ. Such intensity of love is often lacking in today's Christian. To us Hell is often only a category of theology, an academic subject to be discussed. Paul's concern for lost people was an anguish of heart reminiscent of Christ's weeping over the city of Jerusalem (Matthew 23:37) and then suffering judgment for its sin.

I once heard a story about a church that dismissed its pastor because he kept telling the congregation that they were going to Hell. Then their new pastor also told them they were bound for Hell. But they did not have a problem with him. When questioned about the different reactions to the two pastors, one church member replied, "When the first pastor told us we were going to Hell, he sounded like he was glad about it, but when the new pastor says it, he sounds like it breaks his heart." It ought to break our hearts too that people are lost. It should especially break our hearts that Israel is lost.

Why should we grieve over lost Jewish people more than we grieve over other lost people? The reason is not that the souls of Jews are more important, but that they were given unique privileges from which they never benefited. No other nation was ever blessed as Israel was, yet she reaped nothing from her spiritual advantages. Paul's sorrow was over a nation that in spite of her privileges rejected the Messiah.

THE PRIVILEGES OF ISRAEL - ROMANS 9:4-5

In Romans 9:4-5 Paul listed eight unique privileges given only to Israel:

1. Adoption as Sons

God chose to adopt the Jewish people as a nation. This adoption did not mean that every individual Jewish person was His child, but that Israel collectively had a special relationship with God. Moses wrote in Deuteronomy 7:6, "For thou art an holy people unto the Lord thy God; the Lord thy God hath chosen thee to be a special people unto himself, above all people that are upon the face of the earth." In Hosea 11:1 God called Israel His son. Through adoption Israel became the recipients of God's special favor.

2. The Glory

Paul was referring to the *shekinah,* the presence of God in visible manifestation described in Exodus 40:34-38:

> Then a cloud covered the tent of the congregation, and the glory of the Lord filled the tabernacle. And Moses was not able to enter into the tent of the congregation, because the cloud abode thereon, and the glory of the Lord filled the tabernacle. And when the cloud was taken up from over the tabernacle, the children of Israel went onward in all their journeys; But if the cloud were not taken up, then they journeyed not till the day that it was taken up. For the cloud of the Lord was upon the tabernacle by day, and fire was on it by night, in the sight of all the house of Israel, throughout all their journeys.

No nation but Israel had the inestimable privilege of God's visible presence guiding, protecting, and assuring them.

3. The Covenants

God covenanted with Israel's leaders: Abraham, Isaac, Jacob, Moses, and David. He committed Himself to do certain things for Israel which He will never do for any other nation.

4. The Giving of the Law

As Christians we read the law of Moses, but it was not given to us. The law was specifically given only to Israel. Some of the laws of the United States are based upon the law of God, but God never gave His legal code to any nation but Israel.

5. The Temple Service

Only Israel was given the privilege of serving the Lord in the tabernacle and in the temple. The entire system of temple service was a requirement for acceptable worship.

6. The Promises

God gave to Israel the promise of the Messiah's reign and the promise of blessings that will flow from that reign. No other nation has ever been given these promises. All other nations receive their blessings through Israel and Israel's King.

7. The Fathers

The nations of the world can read in the Bible about Abraham, Isaac, and Jacob, but only Israel can claim them as ancestors and the holy roots of its nation.

8. The Messiah

Only of Israel can it be said: "Of whom as concerning the flesh Christ came" (Romans 9:5). The greatest honor and blessing ever given to the nation of Israel was that from its loins came Jesus the Messiah. Jesus was a Jewish man but since He was also God, Paul added, "Who is over all, God blessed for ever."

No other nation has ever been as blessed as Israel. No other people has ever been as privileged as the Jewish people. Yet in spite of her privileges and blessings, she officially rejected Jesus the Messiah. When Christ came to her, she did not want Him (John 1:11). The tragedy is that without possessing a personal relationship with Christ, Israel cannot benefit from her privileges and blessings. Israel's failure to enter into her inheritance, to take advantage of her unique position, broke the apostle Paul's heart. This tragedy should also break the heart of every believer in Christ.

Having forcefully expressed his passion for his kinsmen, the apostle Paul was ready to launch into a defense of God's righteousness in His dealings with Israel.

Chapter 2

THE TRUE ISRAEL

Romans 9:6-13

I f you have trouble understanding some of the apostle Paul's teachings, you aren't alone. Even his apostolic colleague Peter admitted that some of Paul's writings contain "things hard to be understood" (2 Peter 3:16). One of these "things" that are difficult to digest is the doctrine of election. This doctrine states that God chooses to save some people and passes over others, and at first glance the teaching seems unfair and unrighteous. Yet God's election is the teaching Paul presented in Romans 9 to defend God's righteousness in His past dealings with Israel. Paul pointed out that God's sovereignty in choosing some Jewish people for salvation doesn't destroy His righteousness, but rather establishes it.

Paul presented his case along two lines of thought. First, he implied his belief in the principle of election by drawing a distinction between physical and spiritual descendants of Abraham, Isaac, and Jacob. Second, he justified his belief in election by presenting illustrations from Israel's history. Both phases of Paul's presentation were intended to reassure those who were doubting the integrity of God.

THE PRINCIPLE OF ELECTION IMPLIED - ROMANS 9:6

Paul began by articulating what was on the mind of every Jewish believer: "...the word of God hath taken none effect [failed]." From the Jewish Christian's perspective, God's Old Testament promises to Israel appeared to have failed. The word translated "failed" suggests a picture of a ship going off course (Acts 27:17). In classical Greek the word is a nautical term describing a ship being driven off course onto rocks or a sandbar.

Had God's Word been driven off course by Israel's rejection of Jesus the Messiah? Can man frustrate the plan of God and drive it off course by refusing to believe the Word of God? (Today people still wonder.) Do we have a disappointed and dejected God who cannot get people saved and thus accomplish His plan?

The Word of God gave scores of promises of salvation to Israel, but Israel's unbelief left many troubled over the trustworthiness of Scripture. Paul addressed their problem by denying the failure of God's Word and by stating a basic Biblical principle.

Why hadn't the Word of God failed? Paul said, "For they are not all Israel, which are of Israel" (Romans 9:6). This short sentence is of paramount importance. Paul's point was that being a physical descendent of Abraham, Isaac, and Jacob doesn't make one a recipient of God's promises to Israel, since only the spiritual descendants of Abraham, Isaac, and Jacob are the recipients of those promises.

As far as God is concerned, there are two kinds of Jews: physical and spiritual. Physical Jews are biological descendants of Abraham, of his son Isaac, and of his grandson Jacob. Anyone born into a Jewish family is a physical Jew regardless of his religious beliefs. Spiritual Jews, however, are not only biological descendants of Abraham, Isaac, and Jacob, but also spiritual descendants having the same faith as their patriarchal forefathers. A spiritual Jew is a person who has been born into a Jewish family and has trusted Jesus as the Messiah.

Earlier in his letter to the Romans Paul had defined a spiritual Jew by saying, "For he is not a Jew, which is one outwardly; neither is that circumcision, which is outward in the flesh: But he is a Jew, which is one inwardly; and circumcision is that of the heart, in the spirit, and not in the letter; whose praise is not of men, but of God" (2:28-29).

I am Jewish as a result of being born of Jewish parents. For the first eighteen years of my life I was merely a physical Jew, but when I accepted Jesus as my Savior, I became a spiritual Jew also.

What do all these definitions of physical and spiritual Jews have to do with the Word of God not failing? To relieve the anxiety of those who questioned God's integrity in keeping His promises to Israel, Paul was pointing out that the salvation promises God made to Israel are going to be ultimately fulfilled not for physical Jews, but for spiritual Jews.

A parallel situation exists today. Many people consider themselves to be a part of Christendom, but not all of them are true Christians. We could legitimately say that not all Christendom is Christian and therefore the promises of God to His church will only be fulfilled for those who are the true Christians within Christendom. In the same way, not all Israel is Israel, and the promises to the Jewish nation will only be fulfilled for those who are the spiritual seed.

In Christ's day many Jewish people failed to comprehend the distinction between the true spiritual seed and the physical nation of Israel. Jesus had to tell the religious leaders of His day that while they might be the physical descendants of Abraham, they certainly weren't his spiritual children. By their attitudes and actions they reflected their true spiritual father, Satan (John 8:39-44). Like so many people today those religious leaders thought that their physical birth secured their salvation. Personal salvation is an individual matter. A Gentile does not become a Christian by being born into a Christian family any more than a Jewish person becomes a recipient of God's promises to Israel by being born into a Jewish family.

In spite of the fact that the majority of Jewish people rejected the gospel, God could be faithful in keeping His promises to Israel because these promises were never intended for every single Jewish person. They were intended for a select group of Jewish individuals within the nation who were true believers (spiritual Jews). For this small minority God will fulfill every one of His promises.

The Bible refers to these true Israelites as the "remnant" (Romans 9:27; 11:1-5). A *remnant* is something considered an insignificant leftover from the majority. There has always been a remnant of godly Jews—true believers like their father Abraham. In Elijah's day there was a remnant of seven thousand who had not apostatized. In Christ's day there were thousands of Jewish people who followed Him. Today there is an increasing number of Jewish people coming to Jesus the Messiah.

By teaching the principle of a true Israel within a national Israel—a chosen few within the whole—Paul was implying the doctrine of election. Although he did not state the doctrine explicitly, he narrowed down true Israel to a chosen remnant. Teaching this principle, Paul touched upon a sensitive nerve. (Imagine how explosive the reaction of today's Jewish person would be.) When Jesus told the religious leaders of Israel that Abraham wasn't their father, they struck out in anger by calling Him a Samaritan and a demoniac (John 8:48). Therefore in anticipation of his readers' strong reaction to the doctrine of election, Paul took them to their own Scriptures to prove the validity of the concept of an elect Israel within a national Israel.

THE PROOF OF ELECTION ILLUSTRATED - ROMANS 9:7-13

Paul chose two Old Testament examples to illustrate the principle of God's sovereign choice in election: Isaac and Jacob.

The Example of Isaac

Quoting from Genesis 21:12, the apostle wrote:

> Neither, because they are the seed of Abraham, are they
> all children: but, In Isaac shall thy seed be called. That
> is, They which are the children of the flesh, these are
> not the children of God: but the children of the promise
> are counted for the seed. For this is the word of
> promise, At this time will I come, and Sarah shall have
> a son (Romans 9:7-9).

Paul turned to the formation of the Jewish nation to
prove that God's method in dealing with Israel has always
been based on election. While Ishmael and Isaac were both
sons of Abraham, God chose Isaac to be the line through
which the blessings would come. Even though Ishmael was
the older son (thirteen years older) and the natural one to
inherit the promises given by God to Abraham, God sovereignly chose Isaac to inherit those promises. In explaining this
choice of Isaac over Ishmael, commentator Roy E. Gingrich
stated:

> The Lord chose Isaac and not Ishmael to be both a
> child of Abraham and a child of God. Ishmael was a
> child of the flesh, a child of a natural process, a child
> of a fleshly desire. He was not Abraham's child nor
> God's child. Isaac was a child of the flesh and a child
> of the Spirit, a child of a natural process and a child of
> a spiritual process, a child of a fleshly desire and a
> child of a divine promise (he was born by the Spirit in
> fulfillment of a divine promise, a promise by God that
> He would come at His own time and that through His
> own power Isaac would be born, Gen. 18:10). Isaac was
> both a child of Abraham and a child of God.
>   Ishmael and Isaac are types. All of Abraham's

physical descendants who, like Ishmael, are born only of the flesh in fulfillment of a fleshly desire are not the children of Abraham and of God, but all of Abraham's physical descendants who, like Isaac, are born, not only of the flesh in fulfillment of a fleshly desire, but also of the Spirit in fulfillment of a divine promise (a promise to Abraham of a spiritual seed) are the children of Abraham and of God.[1]

Paul was trying to make the point that from the very beginning of Israel's history, God chose some to bless and others not to bless. God never intended for all of the descendants of Abraham to receive the blessings of salvation promised to the children of Abraham.

By choosing Isaac over Ishmael, God established a pattern of election that continues to this day. We don't have to be confused by Israel's rejection of Christ, because not every physical descendant of Abraham has been selected by God to be the recipient of His blessings of salvation. Election has always been the method God uses with the Jewish people, as the choice of Isaac proves.

Someone could object to Paul's use of Isaac as an illustration of election, since Ishmael was not a pure Jew. He was the son of Sarah's handmaid Hagar (Genesis 16:2-4). So Paul used still another Biblical illustration to prove the principle of election.

The Example of Jacob

The apostle cited the case of Isaac's twin boys, Jacob and Esau. Esau was born first, but God chose Jacob. Paul wrote:

When Rebecca also had conceived by one, even by our father Isaac; (For the children being not yet born, neither having done any good or evil, that the purpose of God according to election might stand, not of works, but

of him that calleth;) It was said unto her, The elder
shall serve the younger. As it is written, Jacob have I
loved, but Esau have I hated (Romans 9:10-13).

Why did God choose Jacob over Esau? Was it because
Jacob's character was more righteous than Esau's? Paul de-
nied this line of reasoning by declaring that God's election
was made prior to their births, before they had done anything
good or evil. Is it possible, though, that God looked ahead and
saw what their respective characters would be and based His
choice on His foreknowledge? The Biblical record doesn't
support this theory, for Scripture portrays Jacob as cunning
and deceptive.

The sole reason for God's choice of Jacob over Esau is that
it was God's plan to choose Jacob over Esau. God purposed it
in His heart and then brought it to pass. God's purposes never
fail and His promises never go off course like a ship being
driven onto the rocks. Even if most of Israel has spurned the
Messiah, the chosen remnant will receive the promised salvation.

Paul closed his illustrative arguments with two Old Testament quotes. First, in Romans 9:12 he quoted a statement
made by God in Genesis 25:23 to the mother of Jacob and Esau:
"The elder shall serve the younger." Since nowhere in the
Bible are we ever told that Esau actually served Jacob, this
prediction must go beyond these two individuals.

The complete promise given to Rebecca gives insight into
the true intent of God's statement. In Genesis 25:23 He said,
"Two nations are in thy womb, and two manner of people
shall be separated from thy bowels; and the one people shall
be stronger than the other people; and the elder shall serve the
younger." The key phrase in this verse is "two nations." The
nation that came from Esau was called Edom. Edom became
a nation of idolaters and the enemy of Israel. In judgment,
God made the Edomites servants to the Israelites, who came
from Jacob.

Paul's second Old Testament quote was lifted from a statement made by God more than one thousand years after Jacob and Esau had lived and died. Taken from Malachi 1:2-3, it appears in Romans 9:13: "Jacob have I loved, but Esau have I hated." This amazing statement from the last book of the Old Testament has troubled many unnecessarily. God was not referring to loving Jacob personally while hating Esau personally. God was saying that at the beginning of Israel's history He chose Jacob over Esau before they were born, and at the close of Israel's Old Testament history He could sum up His attitude toward His chosen people as love and His attitude toward the idolatrous nation of Edom as hate.

When we consider the illustrations of Isaac and Jacob, we realize that to deny the doctrine of election would be to deny the history of Israel. Throughout her history God has defined the true Israel as an elect remnant of Jews who are chosen on the basis of divine calling and not on the basis of physical ancestry. Through these elect Jews God fulfills His Word to Israel and thus the doctrine of election establishes the righteousness of God.

---

1. Roy E. Gingrich, *The Great Theodicy of Paul* (Memphis: Riverside, 1986) 7.

Chapter 3

THE RIGHTEOUSNESS OF GOD

Romans 9:14-18

"It's not fair!" Anyone who has raised children is familiar with these words of accusation. It is common for children to accuse parents of unfair treatment. And whenever the doctrine of election is taught, its opponents cry out to their heavenly Father, "It's not fair!" However it is a very serious matter to accuse a righteous God of partiality.

Having just revealed the principle of election, the apostle Paul was certain that some of his readers would have objections. The first objection would come in the form of the question, Does election destroy God's righteousness? Paul's answer to this question is found in Romans 9:14-18. He approached the issue by first stating the accusation of unrighteousness and then answering the charge with an appeal to Scripture.

THE ACCUSATION OF SIN - ROMANS 9:14

With keen insight into the human heart, Paul acknowledged the question on the minds of those who objected to election. He asked, "What shall we say then? Is there unrighteousness with God?" Then he immediately answered the accusation that God is unjust. The very suggestion of God being unjust caused Paul to blurt out, "God forbid."

It is unthinkable that a perfectly holy God could commit

an act of unrighteousness. The psalmist declared that the Lord is upright, having no unrighteousness in Him (Psalm 92:15). God revealed Himself in His law as "a God of truth and without iniquity, just and right" (Deuteronomy 32:4). Abraham acknowledged the justice of God when he rhetorically asked, "Shall not the Judge of all the earth do right?" (Genesis 18:25)

Yet in spite of the numerous Biblical references affirming God's justice, the doctrine of election raises serious doubts in the minds of many people about God's fairness in choosing one person over another. Without a balanced Biblical perspective, the doctrine of election appears to portray God as partial.

THE APPEAL TO SCRIPTURE - ROMANS 9:15-18

To answer the charge against the justice of God, the apostle Paul appealed to the Old Testament Scriptures. Paul didn't attempt to rationalize the doctrine of election, dilute its content, or explain away the obvious meanings of Scripture. Instead his approach was to allow the Bible to speak for itself. Difficulties with the doctrine cannot be resolved in the realm of the intellect. In fact man's intellectual limitations are the very reason people struggle over election. Paul knew we don't have the brain capacity to fully comprehend the doctrine, so he turned to the authority of Scripture to settle the issue.

Having already illustrated the principle of election by the choice of Isaac and Jacob, Paul passed over four hundred years of Jewish history to the time when God gave Moses His law. While Moses was on mount Sinai receiving the law, the children of Israel were participating in the idolatrous worship of a golden calf. As a result of their sin, judgment fell and three thousand people were killed (Exodus 32:28).

Following this severe display of His wrath, God revealed to Moses that he had found favor in His sight. But Moses asked

God to prove it by showing him His glory (Exodus 33:18). God's response to this request is recorded in Exodus 33:19 and quoted by Paul in Romans 9:15: "I will have mercy on whom I will have mercy, and I will have compassion on whom I will have compassion." God's message to Moses was that while all Israel deserved to die, He was a compassionate God who sovereignly bestowed mercy on those He chose. While all Israel deserved to die, God mercifully spared all except three thousand people.

By using this incident in the life of the Hebrew nation, Paul biblically answered the charge of injustice against the doctrine of election. His point was that if anyone dares to accuse God of injustice because He chooses one man over another, the accuser has to conclude that God was unjust when He spared the nation of Israel in the days of Moses. If God had given every Jewish person justice, the Jewish people would have ceased to exist as a nation long ago. Israel owed her survival to God's elective purposes in bestowing compassion upon the nation.

The mercy of God in election goes unnoticed by those who object to the doctrine. They erroneously conclude that by selecting some, God is condemning the rest. But these objectors overlook the fact that the whole human race is already condemned. Since all people are born sinful and condemned before a holy God (Psalm 51:5; Romans 3:23), all deserve judgment. Election does not condemn sinful people; instead it serves to deliver some out of the mass of condemned sinners. Instead of being unfair, election is merciful. To choose to save a man who deserves to die eternally is an act of pure mercy and compassion.

Those who charge God with injustice should keep in mind that He would be absolutely just and fair if He never chose anyone to experience salvation. The fact that He chooses some to be the recipients of saving grace is a reflection of His mercy. If objectors to election want justice, they are looking for it in the wrong place. Justice cannot be found in the doctrine of election because election is a matter of mercy and compassion.

In light of this sovereignly bestowed mercy, it is appropriate to ask, "Why did God choose anybody?" Paul supplied the answer by stating in Romans 9:16, "It is not of him that willeth, nor of him that runneth, but of God that sheweth mercy." God's sovereign choice does not depend on an individual's desire to be shown mercy ("him that willeth") or an individual's efforts to obtain mercy ("him that runneth"). God's choice depends solely on His own will. God determines to whom He will show mercy. Far from denying man's responsibility (which Paul discussed in Romans 10), the apostle was asserting that apart from God's sovereign mercy no man would ever will to be saved. Paul had previously revealed this stunning truth to the Christians at Rome when he wrote, "There is none that seeketh after God." (Romans 3:11).

God has not revealed the basis for His selection of one person over another. However, He has revealed that His choices do not make Him unjust. Being sovereign, He has the right to bestow mercy on whomever He chooses to favor. He also has the right to withhold His mercy from anyone, and instead bestow judgment upon him. Having used Israel and Moses as examples of recipients of mercy, Paul turned to pharaoh as an Old Testament example of a recipient of judgment.

Quoting Exodus 9:16 Paul wrote, "For the scripture saith unto Pharaoh, Even for this same purpose have I raised thee up, that I might shew my power in thee, and that my name might be declared throughout all the earth" (Romans 9:17). According to the Biblical record in Exodus, this particular pharaoh was sovereignly raised up by God during the strategic period of Israel's deliverance from slavery in order to display God's power and proclaim His name throughout the world. That God's purpose for pharaoh was fulfilled is evidenced by the song the children of Israel sang after they crossed the Red Sea; in the song they acknowledged that the nations around them would tremble when they heard of God's deliverance of His people (Exodus 15:14-15). And every year when the Jewish people celebrate the feast of Passover, God's power and name are being proclaimed throughout the world.

Was God unjust because He chose to withhold mercy from pharaoh? The answer is negative because God can do whatever He wants to do and whatever He wants to do is right. This was Paul's point as he brought his defense of God's righteousness to a conclusion: "Therefore hath he mercy on whom he will have mercy, and whom he will he hardeneth" (Romans 9:18). God is perfectly just in choosing to show mercy to one person and in hardening the heart of another by withholding mercy.

We need to be careful not to misunderstand Paul's words concerning God's hardening the heart of pharaoh. The apostle was not teaching that God used pharaoh like a mechanical robot. God did not violate pharaoh's will and force him to do something he never wanted to do. According to the account given in the book of Exodus, God sent Moses to pharaoh with the same message time after time, "Let my people go!" And what was the king of Egypt's response? While at times he appeared to give in to the divine demands, in reality he kept stubbornly refusing to obey.

There are at least fifteen references in Exodus 7–14 to the hardening of pharaoh's heart. Sometimes we read that God hardened it (Exodus 9:12) and sometimes we read that pharaoh hardened it (Exodus 8:15). Who hardened pharaoh's heart? The Biblical answer seems to be that God hardened pharaoh's heart only in the sense that the presentation of righteous commands brought out the evil opposition of the king's heart. In other words, by withholding His mercy God allowed pharaoh's heart to become what pharaoh wanted it to become: harder and harder.

Was God unfair to pharaoh? No! God found pharaoh wicked and rebellious and He simply let him remain in that hardened condition in order to accomplish His sovereign purposes. There is nothing unrighteous in not softening a man's heart. What pharaoh received was the justice he deserved rather than the mercy he did not deserve.

THE APPLICATION TO THE SITUATION

The Jewish people of Paul's day said, "It's not fair that God should choose some Jewish people to be saved while the majority are condemned." Many today spurn the doctrine of election over the same concern for fairness. However pure the motives for rejecting this doctrine may be, election does not detract from the justice of a perfectly righteous God. Election only magnifies His mercy and compassion. The very existence of the church is based on God's mercy in choosing a people to exalt His name.

> But ye are a chosen generation, a royal priesthood, an holy nation, a peculiar people; that ye should shew forth the praises of him who hath called you out of darkness into his marvellous light: Which in time past were not a people, but are now the people of God: which had not obtained mercy, but now have obtained mercy (1 Peter 2:9-10).

Instead of troubling us, the truths about election should cause us to stand in awe of a sovereign God. We will never understand the mysteries behind election. We are unable to comprehend why God chose to display mercy to Moses and not to pharaoh. Both men were sinners. Both men heard God speak and witnessed His miracles. Yet God chose to save Moses and not pharaoh. When we contemplate these mysteries, we should be filled with praise for the mercy of God.

Chapter 4

A THEOLOGICAL PARADOX

Romans 9:19-29

Someone has compared divine election to getting married—you think you are making the choice, but in reality you have already been chosen. We wish that the doctrine of election could be as easily understood as the concept of choosing a spouse. However, election is a Biblical truth that goes beyond man's capacity to grasp.

When the English preacher Charles Spurgeon was asked how he reconciled the doctrines of divine election and human responsibility, he replied, "I don't, for I never try to reconcile friends."[1] While the two doctrines may be friends, many people see them as mortal enemies pitted against each other in a great theological struggle. Whenever the doctrine of election is discussed, an opponent inevitably raises the question, "If God sovereignly elects some to salvation, how can He hold the non-elect responsible for rejecting Him?"

THE CHARGE - ROMANS 9:19

Having answered the charge that election destroys God's righteousness, Paul anticipated a second objection. Some of his readers would claim that election destroys human responsibility. Paul set forth the objection in Romans 9:19: "Thou wilt say then unto me, Why doth he yet find fault? For who hath resisted his will?" On the surface, this appears to be an honest question. However, it expresses the irreverence of those who blame God for holding man responsible for his sin.

Essentially the question is, If God hardens some men, how can He turn around and blame them for being hard? In the case of pharaoh, if God hardened his heart and used him to accomplish His will, how can God be just in punishing him? This is no ordinary question but rather an attempt to blame God for man's sin and thus avoid any personal responsibility. The accusers reason that if God is sovereign, He cannot hold them responsible for resisting His will.

How did Paul deal with such an objection? His approach was not to settle the theological tension that exists between divine sovereignty and human responsibility. He, like Spurgeon, never tried to reconcile friends. Instead he focused on the real issue: the attitude of audacious irreverence on the part of the objectors.

People who dare to accuse God of being unjust because He sovereignly chooses to save some and hold others responsible for their unbelief, have insufficient knowledge about God. They don't understand the God they accuse. Therefore Paul presented truths about the power of God, the purposes of God, and the promises of God—truths that these accusers need to know.

THE POWER OF GOD - ROMANS 9:20-21

First Paul rebuked the irreverence of the spokesman who challenged God's justice and integrity. The apostle wrote, "Nay but, O man, who art thou that repliest against God?" (Romans 9:20) Far from treating this objection to election as a sincere question, Paul treated it as a wicked accusation against God. His response was to condemn the arrogance of the objector by facing him with a question: "Who do you think you are to speak to God this way?" It is obvious from the man's impugning of God's character that he lacked understanding of his frailty in relation to God's exalted authority. He was ignorant of God's power to do whatever He chooses to do with His creatures. Therefore Paul took the opportunity to give this arrogant objector a lesson on the authority of God.

The thrust of Paul's argument centered around the Old Testament imagery of a piece of clay and a potter. He asked, "Shall the thing formed say to him that formed it, Why hast thou made me thus?" (Romans 9:20) Using an analogy familiar to his Jewish readers (see Isaiah 29:16; 45:9; 64:8; Jeremiah 18:6), Paul was comparing God to a potter, and man to a piece of clay. Just as a potter has the right to mold a piece of clay into whatever shape he chooses (without complaint from the clay), so God has the right to do whatever He desires with a man (without disrespectful back talk from him).

We need to be careful that we don't misinterpret Paul's statement. Some Bible teachers, in their zeal to help people with their self-esteem, misapply Romans 9:20. These teachers may say, for example, "If God created you with freckles or a big nose, you have no right to question Him because He knows what He is doing." While it is true that God is in charge of a person's physical appearance, this verse has absolutely nothing to do with God as Creator. Paul did not say, "Shall the thing created say to the Creator...?" He said, "Shall the thing formed say to him that formed it...?"

Why is this distinction so important? The Bible does not teach that God originally created man sinful and that He has a right to create sinful creatures in order to punish them. Adam was created in a state of innocence and he chose to sin. The force of Paul's argument is that God is like a potter working with clay. A potter does not create clay; he takes the clay as he finds it. While God knew man would sin, He did not create him sinful. God is not responsible for man's sin. God has simply taken the lump of clay known as sinful humanity and by sovereign election fashioned some of the clay into vessels that receive mercy.

Paul pressed home the truth of God's authority in Romans

9:21: "Hath not the potter power over the clay, of the same lump to make one vessel unto honour, and another unto dishonour?" No one objects when a potter makes from the same lump of clay a beautiful vase for the living room and an ugly ash tray for the bathroom. In Jeremiah 18 God illustrated His authority over Israel by sending the prophet to observe a potter shaping a piece of clay into whatever object he chose to make. Jeremiah did not object to the potter's authority over the clay. He understood and accepted the analogy.

The objector to election needs to understand that if a human potter can make one vessel for an honorable use and another for a dishonorable use, certainly God Almighty has the right to fashion sinful humanity into vessels of mercy or into hardened sinners. In Romans 9 Paul was really saying, "God had the right to make Moses a vessel of mercy for His use and pharaoh a vessel for wrath."

As forceful as this analogy of potter and clay may be, some may object on the basis that people are different from lumps of clay—human beings have feelings, intelligence, and wills. However, those who object miss the apostle's point. Men and clay are similar in the sense that they are both at the mercy of their masters to make them into whatever He sovereignly wills them to be. The issue is the power and authority of the master, not the makeup of the object molded. Just as the potter has the right to determine the destiny of his clay, so God has the right to determine the destiny of His creatures.

THE PURPOSES OF GOD - ROMANS 9:22-24

Having stated that God is sovereign, like a potter over clay, Paul applied this truth to the way God uses election to work out His eternal purposes. Paul wrote, "What if God, willing to shew his wrath, and to make his power known, endured with much longsuffering the vessels of wrath fitted to destruction" (9:22). A paraphrase of this verse could read, "What if God, even though He desired to send men to Hell for their sin immediately, withheld His judgment and was patient toward those deserving judgment?"

The gist of Romans 9:22 is that God has been very patient with vessels of wrath who oppose, insult, and hate Him. This truth of God's patience with sinners answers two questions: First, why hasn't God wiped out the pagan world that has suppressed His truths revealed in nature (Romans 1)? Second, why didn't God wipe out the entire nation of Israel the moment they worshiped a golden calf (Exodus 32)? The answer to both questions is explicitly stated in Romans 9:23: "That he might make known the riches of his glory on the vessels of mercy, which he had afore prepared unto glory." God has been patient with the world of sinners (both Gentile and Jewish) because out of the clay of sinful humanity He has chosen to save some and take them to glory.

God allows sin and suffering to continue instead of wiping out this rebellious world and sending everyone to Hell. One reason is that He has mercifully chosen some of the rebels to be vessels of mercy. These vessels have been prepared beforehand for glory. They were chosen in Christ before the foundation of the world (Ephesians 1:4). Yet in order for these chosen ones to experience salvation, God continues to endure "with much longsuffering the vessels of wrath fitted to destruction."

Do you know what God is doing in the world today? He is calling out His chosen ones from the lump of humanity. Paul identified these chosen vessels of mercy as "even us, whom he hath called, not of the Jews only, but also of the Gentiles" (Romans 9:24). In the world of pagans and Jews, God is making known the riches of His glory to previously chosen individuals. Peter affirmed this truth when he spoke of the church in these words:

> But ye are a chosen generation, a royal priesthood, an holy nation, a peculiar people; that ye should shew

forth the praises of him who hath called you out of
darkness into his marvellous light: Which in time past
were not a people, but are now the people of God: which
had not obtained mercy, but now have obtained mercy
(1 Peter 2:9-10).

God's eternal purposes are fulfilled through His sovereign
election. Can He legitimately be accused of being unjust
because puny man cannot reconcile divine sovereignty with
human responsibility? The answer is an emphatic no! While
man is mentally incapable of resolving this theological para-
dox, he is capable of understanding that the truths about the
nature of God ought to silence his arrogant accusation.

THE PROMISES OF GOD - ROMANS 9:25-29

In Romans 9:25-29 the apostle Paul quoted two Old Testament prophets, Hosea and Isaiah, to prove that God's messengers predicted that salvation would come to only a chosen
minority of the Hebrew nation. The truth of sovereign election
is soundly based on the promises of God as revealed through
the ancient prophets.

The Prophet Hosea

Referring first to a promise in the book of Hosea, Paul
wrote: "As he saith also in [Hosea], I will call them my people,
which were not my people; and her beloved, which was not
beloved. And it shall come to pass, that in the place where it
was said unto them, Ye are not my people; there shall they be
called the children of the living God" (Romans 9:25-26).

In the book of Hosea Israel is depicted as the idolatrous
and unfaithful wife of Jehovah. As a result of her sin, she is on
the verge of being taken captive by the empire of Assyria. God
sent Hosea to be His spokesman to the adulterous nation of
Israel. However, Hosea was more than a messenger to his

people, for he was made a living illustration portraying God's love toward Israel. Hosea married a prostitute, Gomer (Hosea 1:2-3), and their relationship became a picture of God's relationship to Israel. Hosea as the loving husband represented God, and Gomer as the adulterous wife represented Israel.

When Gomer's second and third children were born, God told Hosea to give them names that expressed His dismay with Israel's behavior. The second child was named *Lo-ruhamah* (Hosea 1:6), which means "unpitied" and "no mercy." The name indicated that as a result of Israel's sin, God would remove His compassion from the nation. He would have no pity on Israel. The third child was named *Lo-ammi* (Hosea 1:9), which means "not my people" or "no kin of mine." This name indicated that God would sever His relationship with unfaithful Israel. Yet the Lord mercifully promised to restore Israel to His favor.

However, this promise of mercy is reserved only for a remnant within the nation of Israel. To develop his point concerning mercy for the remnant, Paul quoted from the book of Isaiah.

The Prophet Isaiah

Quoting the promise in Isaiah 10:22-23, Paul wrote: "[Isaiah] also crieth concerning Israel, Though the number of the children of Israel be as the sand of the sea, a remnant shall be saved: For he will finish the work, and cut it short in righteousness: because a short work will the Lord make upon the earth" (Romans 9:27-28). Isaiah predicted that although the population of Israel was considerable, only a minority of the Israelites would survive the Assyrian captivity and return physically to Israel and spiritually to God. While the number of Israelites was like the sand of the sea, God promised to save only a remnant. His mercy would extend to only a chosen few.

What if God had not promised to save a remnant of Jewish

people? Paul once again turned to the prophet Isaiah to answer
that question. Quoting Isaiah 1:9 the apostle wrote, "And as
[Isaiah] said before, Except the Lord of Sabaoth had left us a
seed, we had been as Sodoma, and been made like unto
Gomorrha" (Romans 9:29). Sodom and Gomorrah were ancient cities noted for their wickedness. In Genesis 18 God told
Abraham that He would preserve these cities from judgment if
ten righteous citizens could be found. However because a
godly remnant of that number did not exist in Sodom and
Gomorrah, God completely annihilated those cities.

In Isaiah's day Israel was in a state of wicked rebellion.
She was a "sinful nation, a people laden with iniquity, a seed
of evildoers" (Isaiah 1:4). She was spiritually diagnosed as
having a sick head, a faint heart, and a body full of bruises,
welts, and raw wounds (1:5-6). To this corrupt people Isaiah
announced that their fate was not the same as that of Sodom
and Gomorrah only because they possessed something those
cities lacked: a godly remnant.

Paul was making the same point as the Old Testament
prophet. The survival of the Jewish people is rooted in the fact
that God has preserved for Himself a chosen remnant within
the nation of Israel. Had God withheld His mercy and not
saved some chosen Israelites, the nation would have been
completely destroyed. No one can legitimately complain
about Israel not being saved. Election of a Jewish remnant is
the means by which the nation has been physically spared.

What tremendous implications this truth has for us today.
Hebrew Christians are often rejected and ostracized by the
Jewish community. They are falsely accused of no longer
being Jewish and charged with attempting to destroy the
Jewish people by their evangelistic efforts. Yet according to
the prophet Isaiah and the apostle Paul, Hebrew Christians, as
the remnant, are the very reason the Jewish people have been
preserved. Far from destroying Israel, Jewish believers form
the basis for Israel's continued survival. How ironic it is that

the people considered a threat to the Jewish community are in reality the very reason the Jewish community continues to exist.

God could have and would have destroyed Israel long ago, except that He has a chosen remnant to save. Today He continues to preserve the Jewish people in order that the remainder of the remnant will be saved. This truth should encourage every Christian involved in Jewish evangelism, for the implication is that some Jewish people *will* turn to Christ. In a ministry that does not often yield significant results, it is important to remember that God has promised to save some Jewish people. While the majority will continue in unbelief, God will always have a remnant of Hebrew believers who have faith in Him.

Down through the centuries God has preserved for Himself a remnant of godly Jewish people. The history of the Jewish nation reveals that there were always a faithful few who walked with the Lord in obedience. Even during the darkest days of apostasy, God reminded the prophet Elijah of seven thousand Israelites "all the knees which have not bowed unto Baal" (1 Kings 19:18; also see Romans 11:4). It is no coincidence that every generation has some Jewish people who know the Lord. The remnant is result of God's promise to extend mercy to a chosen few.

In focusing on Old Testament promises of God's mercy to a chosen remnant, Paul taught his arrogant challenger (Romans 9:19) a vital truth about God: God keeps His promises. To any individual who complains that election is unfair to the nonelect, Paul's answer is that election does not destroy anyone; rather it fulfills God's promise of mercy to a chosen remnant. The irreverent man who dared to accuse God of being unjust failed to understand that a chosen remnant is a fulfillment of God's promise. Far from suggesting the failure of God's Word, an elect remnant proves the faithfulness of God's Word.

The accuser's objection that God hardens a man's heart and then holds him responsible for his hardness, was not dealt with by Paul in Romans 9:19-29. Instead Paul focused on the character of the God who elects. As difficult as the truth about God's hardening people may be, it must be understood that people are not lost because God hardens them. His hardening process doesn't make them unbelievers. Because they are already willfully hardened unbelievers, God hardens them more—as He did in pharaoh's case.

No one is lost because he is elected to be lost. In the Bible *election* and *predestination* refer only to the saved (or those who will be saved). These terms never refer to the unsaved. No one is ever predestined to Hell. Yet the question remains, why are people lost? More specifically, why were the vast majority of Jewish people of Paul's day lost? Paul answered this question in Romans 10, where he looked at Israel's present condition.

---

1. J. I. Packer, *Evangelism and the Sovereignty of God* (Downers Grove, IL: InterVarsity Press, 1961) 35.

Part Two

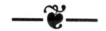

ISRAEL: THE PRESENT

Chapter 5

THE UNBELIEF OF ISRAEL

Romans 9:30–10:1

W hy did the Jewish people of Christ's day reject Him? Many Christians are puzzled over the fact that although Israel knew the Old Testament Messianic prophecies, witnessed the miracles of Jesus, and heard the testimony of gospel witnesses, the nation still did not embrace Jesus as Messiah and King. Instead they despised Him and refused to have Him reign over them. One of the saddest verses in the Bible states, "He came unto his own, and his own received him not" (John 1:11).

Israel's rejection of Christ is the subject of the closing section of Romans 9 and all of Romans 10. After stating in the preceding verses that God has fulfilled His word to Israel through an elect remnant, the apostle Paul began in Romans 9:30 to explain why the majority of Israelites are lost. Their rejection of Christ has nothing to do with sovereign election, but rather with their own unbelief. The doctrine of election only explains why a remnant of Jewish people do believe in Christ. The doctrine doesn't answer the question, Why do most Jewish people not believe in Christ? Therefore Paul shifted his attention from divine election to human responsibility. In Romans 9:30–10:1 the apostle focused on the reality of Israel's unbelief, the reason for her unbelief, and the appropriate response to her unbelief.

THE REALITY OF ISRAEL'S UNBELIEF - ROMANS 9:30-31

First Paul made it clear that the vast majority of Jewish people in his day were characterized by unbelief. In contrast to Gentiles who had trusted Christ, Israelites who had rejected Him were not in a right relationship with God. Paul wrote, "What shall we say then? That the Gentiles, which followed not after righteousness, have attained to righteousness, even the righteousness which is of faith. But Israel, which followed after the law of righteousness, hath not attained to the law of righteousness" (Romans 9:30-31).

The vast majority of Gentiles in Paul's day were not interested in righteousness. Their lifestyles were often immoral. Their large cities were centers of idolatry, sexual perversion, and superstition. In other letters Paul said that Gentiles were characterized by lustful passions (1 Thessalonians 4:5), futility of mind, ignorance, hardness of heart, callousness, sensuality, and greediness (Ephesians 4:17-19). These first-century pagans were certainly not in pursuit of righteousness, yet when they heard the gospel of Christ, many of them received it.

In city after city around the Roman empire Paul found the minds of many Gentiles open to Christ, while the minds of most of his Jewish kinsmen were closed. For instance, at Pisidian Antioch the Jewish community instigated a persecution against Paul and his companion Barnabas, yet a number of Gentiles rejoiced and believed the word of God (Acts 13:44-52). At Thessalonica after some Gentiles were persuaded to believe in Christ, many Jewish people were jealous and started a riot (Acts 17:1-9). Throughout Paul's ministry the pattern remained the same: Gentiles, who once were not interested in righteousness, were open to the gospel's offer of righteousness; and Jews, who had spent their lives trying to attain an acceptable level of righteousness, closed their minds to the gospel.

Jewish people, regardless of their religious zeal, are lost

apart from faith in Christ. When I was a new believer in the Lord, I struggled over this issue. My grandfather, who was an orthodox Jew with a deep belief in the existence of God, spent his entire life observing religious rituals and practices. Yet according to Romans 9:31, although he pursued the law of righteousness, he did not arrive at that law. Even though he worked at being good enough to get into Heaven, he never achieved his goal.

It is important for Bible-believing people to understand that Jewish people, as well as Gentiles, are not saved unless they trust Jesus Christ as their Savior. It is a popular ploy of television talk-show hosts to put evangelical guests on the spot by asking them, "Will Jews go to Hell because they don't believe in Christ?" The answer is that both Jews and Gentiles will spend eternity in Hell unless they trust Christ as Savior. The apostle Peter boldly declared to a group of first-century Jewish leaders, "Neither is there salvation in any other: for there is none other name under heaven given among men, whereby we must be saved" (Acts 4:12).

The Jewish people of Christ's day had religious fervor. Many in Israel, like Nicodemus (John 3), wanted to be righteous enough to enter into the kingdom of God. However when Jesus the Messiah presented Himself as God's provision for their need of righteousness, the majority violently rejected Him.

THE REASON FOR ISRAEL'S UNBELIEF - ROMANS 9:32-33

Israel did not live up to the law of righteousness. Why? Paul declared, "Because they sought it not by faith, but as it were by the works of the law. For they stumbled at that stumblingstone" (Romans 9:32). The typical Jewish person sought righteousness by doing good works. He rejected God's way of obtaining righteousness through faith. He insisted on trying to earn his way to Heaven by obeying the Mosaic law, and it was this determination that caused him to trip over

Christ and the simplicity of the gospel of grace. The typical Jew thought he was too good to need a Savior from sin.

This self-righteous attitude still prevails among most Jewish people (as well as most Gentiles) today. They see themselves as upright, responsible citizens whose good deeds will earn them favor with God. They are insulted when they are told that they are sinners. They disregard Isaiah 53:6: "All we like sheep have gone astray; we have turned every one to his own way." Like the ancient Jewish "sheep" of the prophet Isaiah's day, modern Jews continue to live independent of the Shepherd of Israel. They fail to see that the essence of sin begins with an attitude of independence toward God's right to rule over their lives and manifests itself in actions of disobedience to God's Word.

Instead of leaning on Christ and the righteousness He provides, Israel stumbled over Him. Their pride caused them to insist on earning salvation, rather than receiving it by faith in the crucified Messiah. Their rejection of Christ is even more tragic because their Hebrew Scriptures (Isaiah 8:14; 28:16) foretold this stumbling stone. Paul said, "As it is written, Behold, I lay in [Zion] a stumblingstone and rock of offence: and whosoever believeth on him shall not be ashamed" (Romans 9:33).

The reason Israel continues in their lost state is that they refuse to trust Christ for their salvation. Unlike repentant Gentiles who acknowledge their wickedness and humbly admit their need for righteousness, Israel's pride blinds them to their spiritual need. With heads held high, they fail to notice the Rock God has placed in their path, and consequently they stumble over Him.

THE RESPONSE TO ISRAEL'S UNBELIEF - ROMANS 10:1

What should be our attitude toward unbelieving Jews? Should we ignore them and neglect them in our missionary endeavors? Should we write Israel off as having missed their opportunity to believe? The only acceptable response to Jewish unbelief is revealed in Paul's attitude toward Israel. He wrote, "Brethren, my heart's desire and prayer to God for Israel is, that they might be saved" (Romans 10:1). To Paul the salvation of Israel was a burden. In spite of Israel's rebelliousness toward Christ, the apostle yearned for his people's salvation. Paul's interest in Israel's salvation was more than a professional theologian's concern. His interest was the heartfelt desire of a compassionate man.

This inner desire manifested itself in prayer for the salvation of Israel. Unlike some modern-day believers, Paul never allowed the truth of sovereign election to destroy his prayer life. He never reasoned, "Why bother to pray? If God saves whomever He chooses to save, how can my prayers be of any consequence?" Paul did not see any inconsistency between prayer and the doctrine of sovereign election.

Divine sovereignty is not a deterrent to prayer, but an incentive to ask God to save people, for only a sovereign God is powerful enough to overcome the hardness of men's hearts and bring them to salvation. Sovereign election does not eliminate the need to pray for Jewish people to be saved. We need to keep in mind that God chooses not only the elect remnant, but also the means by which they will come to faith in the Lord. The means God has provided are the Word of God and prayer.

While Paul was anticipating his own execution, he said to Timothy: "I suffer trouble, as an evil doer, even unto bonds; but the word of God is not bound. Therefore I endure all things for the elect's sakes, that they may also obtain the salvation which is in Christ Jesus with eternal glory" (2 Timothy 2:9-10). Paul suffered for the cause of Christ and even risked his life by continuing to preach the gospel because he knew that the elect come to faith in Christ through an understanding of God's Word. Paul declared the significance of the Word of God in bringing the elect to salvation when he said, "So then faith cometh by hearing, and hearing by the word of God" (Romans 10:17).

The Word of God is not the only means by which God has chosen to save the elect. He burdens people to pray for the salvation of the lost. A number of years ago when my mother was dying of lung cancer, the Lord burdened many people at the church I pastor to pray for her salvation. I am convinced that God placed this burden on their hearts as His method of bringing one of His elect to salvation because five hours before she passed away, she placed her trust in Jesus as her Messiah and Savior.

How should we respond to Israel's unbelief? We should desire their salvation, pray for their salvation, and lovingly tell them about the Messiah who offers them salvation through faith, not works.

Chapter 6

THE RESPONSIBILITY OF ISRAEL

Romans 10:2-21

One evidence of the inspiration and inerrancy of the Word of God is its apparent contradictions. The apparent conflicts indicate that God is the author of Scripture. If men had written the Bible on their own initiative, they would have smoothed out its difficulties and seeming discrepancies.

Actually the Bible contains no contradictions; the apparent conflicts are only theological tensions that cannot be resolved by human minds.

Perhaps the most noted theological tension in the Bible is the apparent conflict between divine sovereignty and human responsibility. The Bible teaches that salvation is totally of God and man is incapable of coming to Christ on his own initiative; yet the Bible also calls men to believe in Christ and says they will be held responsible if they do not believe. We are naturally inclined to try to resolve this tension, but the Bible doesn't. This tension stands as a testimony to the Bible's divine origin.

Romans 9–10 demonstrates God's approach to the tension existing between divine sovereignty and human responsibility. First Paul emphasized the sovereignty of God in choosing a handful of Jewish people to be saved. Then he shifted gears to deal with the other side of the coin of salvation: human responsibility.

The purpose of Romans 10 is to prove that the nation of Israel is responsible for her unbelief. Neither God nor the doctrine of election is responsible for Israel's lack of faith in Jesus. Paul presented the reasons why Israel must be blamed for not being saved: salvation has been provided; salvation has been possible; and salvation has been proclaimed.

SALVATION HAS BEEN PROVIDED - ROMANS 10:2-5

Romans 10 opens with an expression of Paul's heartfelt concern and prayer for Israel's salvation (10:1). Paul was burdened for Israel's salvation because he understood her true spiritual condition. He wrote: "For I bear them record that they have a zeal of God, but not according to knowledge. For they being ignorant of God's righteousness, and going about to establish their own righteousness, have not submitted themselves unto the righteousness of God" (10:2-3).

The Jewish people of Paul's day had an incredible zeal for God. They were known as "the God-intoxicated people." Their entire lives were centered around their religion. It was this religious zeal that drove Paul, before his conversion, to kill and persecute Christians (Philippians 3:6). Israel was religiously fanatic, but their zeal wasn't based on a full understanding of the Hebrew Scriptures. Although they were familiar with God's Word, they misunderstood the intention of His law. They believed they could establish their own righteousness by obeying the numerous Biblical commands. Their zeal for good works stemmed from an ardent attempt to be in right relation to God.

This type of religious fervor still characterizes orthodox Jews. For example my grandparents, who were Russian Jews, were deeply committed to their beliefs and in spite of moving to a new world, clung tenaciously to their old ways. They attended synagogue regularly, observed their traditions meticulously, and although it required more work, kept a strict kosher home (they had one set of dishes for meat and another set of dishes for dairy products). Their refusal to work on the sabbath (they considered traveling by automobile to be work) forced my parents to schedule my bar mitzvah (the ceremony celebrating a Jewish boy's becoming a man) on a Monday, rather than the customary Saturday.

In spite of Israel's great zeal, the apostle Paul knew they lacked God's righteousness. Their lack was due to their own ignorance—not an ignorance stemming from innocence or sincerity, but a culpable and willful ignorance. Paul appropriately described their ignorance when he said that they did not submit themselves to the righteousness of God. Their ignorance was caused by rebellion to God's plan of salvation.

The Jewish people of Paul's day chose to ignore their own Scriptures, which revealed God's provision of righteousness. Every time an Israelite read of an animal sacrifice, he should have been reminded of the fact that fellowship with God is only made possible by a payment for sin, not by zealous works. Every time an Israelite participated in the temple sacrifices, he should have been reminded of the fact that "it is the blood that maketh an atonement for the soul" (Leviticus 17:11). And when Jesus was identified as "the Lamb of God" (John 1:29) and He died in the manner of a sheep led to the slaughter (Isaiah 53:7), Israel should have recognized Him as God's provision for their need of righteousness.

In light of Israel's stubborn ignorance of God's provision of righteousness Paul boldly declared, "Christ is the end of the law for righteousness to every one that believeth" (Romans 10:4). Because of Jesus Christ everyone can stop trying to attain righteousness. When a person looks at the law properly, he sees himself as unrighteous because he has violated its holy standard (Romans 3:20; 7:7). In brokenness he comes to Christ as God's provision for righteousness. Paul wrote, "He hath made him to be sin for us, who knew no sin; that we might be made the righteousness of God in him" (2 Corinthians 5:21).

While the Jewish remnant submitted to God's plan to give them righteousness by faith in Jesus Christ, the majority of Israelites rejected Him. Stubbornly they clung to their zealous efforts to establish their own righteousness.

It was an impossibility for these Jewish people to attain righteousness by works. Paul expressed the futility of their attempts when he wrote, "Moses describeth the righteousness which is of the law, That the man which doeth those things shall live by them" (Romans 10:5). Quoting Leviticus 18:5, Paul was using the words of the lawgiver to prove that righteousness could not be attained by lawkeeping since the law demanded perfect obedience. James declared the same truth when he wrote, "Whosoever shall keep the whole law, and yet offend in one point, he is guilty of all" (James 2:10). If a person is going to get to Heaven by observing the law, there is no room for error. He must keep all the laws at all times—which is a human impossibility.

Israel's lost condition is not God's fault. The Father sent the Lord Jesus to the lost sheep of the house of Israel, but they rejected Him. He came unto His own, but His own did not receive Him. In spite of having God's provision of righteousness through faith clearly spelled out in the Hebrew Scriptures, the Jewish people of Paul's day rejected God's provision in Christ. In the final analysis Israel is responsible for her unbelief. God is absolved from any blame because He has provided a salvation the Jewish nation should have accepted.

However, remembering the truths about election, some people might wonder if Israel *could* have accepted Christ. Was salvation out of their reach? Was salvation possible for them or did sovereign election make it impossible?

SALVATION HAS BEEN POSSIBLE - ROMANS 10:6-13

In Deuteronomy 30 Moses gave a charge to the children of Israel. After clearly explaining God's will to them, he told them that there would be blessings if they obeyed the Lord and chastisement if they disobeyed Him. Then he said:

> This commandment which I command thee this day, it is not hidden from thee, neither is it far off. It is not in heaven, that thou shouldest say, Who shall go up for us to heaven, and bring it unto us, that we may hear it, and do it? Neither is it beyond the sea, that thou shouldest say, Who shall go over the sea for us, and bring it unto us, that we may hear it, and do it? But the word is very nigh unto thee, in thy mouth, and in thy heart, that thou mayest do it (Deuteronomy 30:11-14).

The meaning of these words of Moses can be summed up this way: The knowledge of God's will is now accessible to you. You are not required to do the impossible, such as ascend to Heaven or go beyond the sea. God's will is not unreachable. You do not have to go searching for something you cannot possibly attain!

These words of Moses were quoted by Paul to prove the possibility of salvation by faith. The apostle wrote:

> The righteousness which is of faith speaketh on this wise, Say not in thine heart, Who shall ascend into heaven? (that is, to bring Christ down from above:) Or, Who shall descend into the deep? (that is, to bring up Christ again from the dead.) But what saith it? The word is nigh thee, even in thy mouth, and in thy heart: that is, the word of faith, which we preach (Romans 10:6-8).

Paul was applying the language of Deuteronomy 30 to Christ. Paul's point was that righteousness by faith does not require us to scale the heavens to bring Christ down. Nor does it require us to go into Hades to raise Him from the dead. Both are impossibilities! The message of salvation is not far away and beyond reach. It is so near to us that it is actually in our mouths and hearts.

How was the gospel close to the Jewish people of Paul's day? The message about Jesus was the talk of every synagogue. Paul's preaching had so turned the world upside down that Jewish people across the Roman empire were discussing the matter. God cannot be blamed for Israel's unbelief. Salvation by faith was within their reach. Unlike salvation by lawkeeping, salvation by faith was possible and available to Israel.

Salvation is available to anyone who will meet the one requirement of faith. Paul wrote, "If thou shalt confess with thy mouth the Lord Jesus, and shalt believe in thine heart that God hath raised him from the dead, thou shalt be saved. For with the heart man believeth unto righteousness; and with the mouth confession is made unto salvation" (Romans 10:9-10). All a person needs to do to be saved from the penalty of sin is to trust that Jesus Christ rose from the dead. Since it is the resurrection that confirmed the person and work of Christ, faith in His resurrection means a heart-trust in Jesus Christ as the God-man who paid the full penalty of sin.

We must not misunderstand the relationship between confession with our mouths and faith in our hearts. Paul did not teach that public confession of Jesus must be made before a person can be saved. Paul mentioned confession before belief only because they were mentioned in that order by Moses. Faith in Christ is the only requirement for salvation. However, true faith in Christ will be expressed by confessing Jesus as Lord. If a person's heart trusts Christ, he'll have to express that faith with his mouth because the heart and the mouth work in harmony. Jesus said, "Out of the abundance of the heart the mouth speaketh" (Matthew 12:34).

Just as Moses had told Israel that God's will was not beyond their reach, so Paul revealed that salvation for Israel was not an impossibility. Salvation was simply a matter of faith. Quoting Isaiah 28:16 to support his point, the apostle wrote, "The scripture saith, Whosoever believeth on him shall not be ashamed" (Romans 10:11).

All that Jewish people need to do to obtain eternal salvation is to trust Jesus. And the invitation to believe is extended beyond Israel, as it also calls Gentiles to faith in Christ. Paul wrote, "There is no difference between the Jew and the Greek: for the same Lord over all is rich unto all that call upon him. For whosoever shall call upon the name of the Lord shall be saved" (Romans 10:12-13; also see Joel 2:32). Righteousness is available from the Lord, who abounds in riches, to whoever calls upon His name for salvation.

The invitation to come to Christ is open to both Jews and Gentiles. However, while all are invited, only the elect will come. This truth brings together both divine sovereignty and human responsibility.

God should never be blamed for a man's refusal to come to Him. God made it possible to be saved. He simply calls you to come to Him in faith. If you want salvation, you can come to Him—today!

SALVATION HAS BEEN PROCLAIMED - ROMANS 10:14-21

"I didn't hear you!" Those were probably the words I spoke most often during my early school years. There was nothing wrong with my ears. My hearing wasn't impaired. I simply chose to let my mind wander and not pay attention to my teachers. However it wasn't long before I realized that my lack of hearing wasn't accepted as a valid excuse. My teachers held me responsible for doing the work they had assigned.

Similarly in Paul's day the nation of Israel was told the gospel message, but they claimed not to have heard it. They tried to blame God for their unbelief, contending that the Lord never sent gospel witnesses to the Jewish people. However, the apostle Paul refused that excuse as invalid. His message in Romans 10:14-21 was that the people of Israel

were responsible for their unbelief because although witnesses had proclaimed salvation, the nation did not believe
the message! The apostle stated three truths that condemn the
nation for their unbelief.

1. Israel Had the Opportunity to Believe - Romans 10:14-15

By asking a series of questions, the apostle argued that
Israel had the opportunity to call upon Christ, but refused to
call upon Him. Since no one can call upon Christ without first
believing in Him, Paul began his argument by asking, "How
then shall they call on him in whom they have not believed?"
(Romans 10:14). Behind the act of calling upon the Lord,
stands the attitude of believing the Lord. Hebrews 11:6 states,
"Without faith it is impossible to please him: for he that
cometh to God must believe that he is, and that he is a
rewarder of them that diligently seek him." Before a person
can call upon Christ, he must first believe that He exists and
that calling upon Him will be beneficial. There must be an
attitude of confidence in Christ in the heart before the mouth
will utter a prayer of salvation.

Although believing in Christ precedes calling upon
Him, no one can believe in Him until he has first heard
about Him. Therefore Paul next asked, "How shall they
believe in him of whom they have not heard?" (Romans
10:14) And since no one can hear the gospel until it is
proclaimed, the apostle appropriately asked, "How shall
they hear without a preacher?" (10:14)

Paul's logic is indisputable. No one can call upon Christ
unless he believes the truth about Him. No one can believe the
truth about Him unless he hears the truth about Him. And no
one can hear that message unless it is proclaimed. If men are
to hear the gospel, heralds must be sent. Therefore Paul
concluded his set of questions by asking, "How shall they
preach, except they be sent?" (10:15).

Paul's purpose in raising these rhetorical questions was to

allow his readers to conclude that no one can call upon the
Lord unless God initiates the salvation process by sending
messengers to proclaim the gospel. If messengers were not
sent by God to the Jewish people, Israel cannot legitimately be
blamed for her unbelief. However, if God did send gospel
witnesses to Israel, the nation stands responsible for her
refusal to call upon Christ for salvation.

The bottom line in the apostle's reasoning is whether or
not the Lord sent messengers to the Jewish people. Quoting
Isaiah 52:7 in his answer, Paul wrote, "How beautiful are the
feet of them that preach the gospel of peace, and bring glad
tidings of good things!" (Romans 10:15). During the closing
days of the Hebrew nation's exile in Babylon, messengers
carried the good news home to Jerusalem that the captivity was
almost over. Isaiah called the feet of those messengers beautiful because their feet enabled them to carry and deliver
wonderful news. Paul's point in Romans 10:15 is obvious: Just
as messengers in Old Testament times published the good
news to Israel concerning the end of their captivity, so messengers in New Testament times were sent to Israel to announce
the good news of salvation in Christ.

The Jewish people of Paul's day had ample opportunity to
hear the gospel. Jesus came solely to the lost sheep of the
house of Israel (Matthew 15:24). The first gospel witnesses
were sent to Israel (Acts 1:8). These witnesses were so ab-
sorbed in their outreach to Israel that at first they didn't realize
that salvation was for Gentiles as well (Acts 10). The early
church was born Jewish as three thousand Hebrew people
from around the Roman empire heard and responded to the
gospel on the day of Pentecost (Acts 2). Israel wasn't neglected
in God's program of gospel proclamation.

Unfortunately although the Jewish people of Paul's day
heard the truth of the Messiah, the majority of today's Jewish
population have never heard a clear presentation of the
gospel. They don't own a New Testament and rarely read the

Old Testament. They don't frequent churches to hear about Christ. They don't watch Christian television or listen to Christian radio. To use Paul's words, "How shall they hear without a preacher? And how shall they preach, except they be sent?"

Jewish people won't hear the gospel unless we tell them about Christ. Jewish people are certainly not the only ones we are to witness to, but we must be careful not to neglect them either. We have been commissioned to take the gospel to the world, which includes Jewish people. We need to have the same missionary concern that consumed the first-century witnesses to Israel. That generation of Israelites had the opportunity to hear the gospel and therefore could not blame God for their unbelief.

2. Israel Rejected the Gospel - Romans 10:16-17

Even though the people of Israel were given the opportunity to respond properly to Christ, they rejected His offer of salvation. Paul wrote, "But they have not all obeyed the gospel. For [Isaiah] saith, Lord, who hath believed our report?" (Romans 10:16) Israel should have viewed the feet of the men and women who brought them the message of Messiah as beautiful and bearers of good news. Instead the Israelites attacked the messengers and rejected the message.

In Romans 10:16 Paul was quoting Isaiah 53:1. Seven hundred years before Christ was born, the prophet Isaiah predicted that his nation would not believe the news reported to them about the suffering Messiah. In essence Isaiah said, "Lord, hardly anyone is going to believe this man is the Messiah." The prophet was correct, for most did not receive Him (John 1:11); only the elect remnant did (John 1:12).

Although the Jewish people of Paul's day were given the opportunity to hear the gospel, they opposed it. Paul's desire was to back the Jewish nation into a corner so that they would have to admit that they, not God, were to blame for their unbelief. So Paul concluded his argument by writing, "So then faith cometh by hearing, and hearing by the word of God" (Romans 10:17). Since faith comes by hearing God's Word about Christ, and Israel had heard about Christ, the Israelites were guilty.

3. Israel Rejected Christ - Romans 10:18-20

Paul won his argument in Romans 10:16-17. He proved his point by using the Jewish Scriptures and sanctified logic. However, he anticipated that Jewish unbelievers would protest his indictment of Israel. Characteristic of his literary style, he quoted an imaginary protester in Romans 10:18-20. This protester raised two objections to the assertion that Israel could have believed the gospel.

The first objection questioned Paul's contention that Israel had heard the gospel: "But I say, Have they not heard? (10:18). Paul responded by stating, "Yes verily, their sound went into all the earth, and their words unto the ends of the world." Paul was using the language of Psalm 19:4 to affirm that just as the heavens declare to all creation the message of God's glory, so gospel witnesses declared salvation in Christ to the Jewish world. If Jewish people did not respond to Jesus, the reason was not that they had never heard the truth. One Bible scholar who caught the gist of Paul's use of Psalm 19 said, "The opportunity of hearing was as wide as the star-studded heavens."[1]

The second objection raised by the imaginary protester attempted to excuse Israel's unbelief on the basis of a lack of understanding: "But I say, Did not Israel know?" (10:19) Did Israel not comprehend the gospel? Did the Jewish people reject Christ because they did not know what He was saying? Did God make the gospel too difficult for Jewish people to understand?

The apostle responded by referring to the Hebrew Scriptures. Quoting Deuteronomy 32:21 Paul wrote, "Moses saith,

I will provoke you to jealousy by them that are no people, and by a foolish nation I will anger you" (Romans 10:19). Quoting Isaiah 65:1 Paul added, "But [Isaiah] is very bold, and saith, I was found of them that sought me not; I was made manifest unto them that asked not after me" (Romans 10:20). Both Moses and Isaiah predicted that Gentiles, who had little understanding of Biblical truth and who did not seek God, would comprehend the gospel of Christ. Paul's point was that if unenlightened pagans can understand the simple gospel, Israel's unbelief cannot be attributed to her lack of understanding the message of salvation.

Israel's problem with Christ did not stem from her lack of hearing or understanding the truth about Him. Her rejection of Christ was due to her stubborn disobedience of God. Paul closed Romans 10 by once again quoting the Old Testament. Citing Isaiah 65:2 the apostle wrote, "To Israel he saith, All day long I have stretched forth my hands unto a disobedient and gainsaying people" (Romans 10:21). The reason Israel did not call upon the Lord for salvation is that she spurned God's love. Yet in spite of her stubbornness, God continues to stretch out His hands, inviting Israel to come to Him. Someday the Jewish nation will accept that invitation and come running to Him (Romans 11). Today He invites all to call upon the name of the Lord for salvation. Have you called upon Him?

-----

1. James Stifler, *The Epistle to the Romans* (Chicago: Moody Press, 1983) 143.

Part Three

ISRAEL: THE PROSPECTS

Chapter 7

HAS GOD REJECTED ISRAEL?

Romans 11:1-10

Has God rejected Israel? For nearly two thousand years people have been asking this question and the majority in Christendom have answered yes. Their affirmative response indicates that they believe that all the promises given to Israel in the Hebrew Scriptures have been canceled and transferred to the church. In contrast to the majority, the apostle Paul answered the question with a stirring "God forbid" (Romans 11:1). In the strongest language possible Paul affirmed that God is not through with Israel.

During this church age, in one sense Israel has been set aside. However this setting aside is not final. God has not permanently rejected the Jewish people and canceled His promises to them. In Romans 11:1-10 Paul argued that in spite of Israel's rejection of Jesus as Messiah, God did not reject the nation. The apostle presented his own conversion, the chosen remnant, and the condition of Israel as evidence to prove that God has not cast away His people.

THE CONVERSION OF PAUL - ROMANS 11:1

Paul presented himself as the first line of evidence that God has not rejected Israel. The apostle wrote, "For I also am an Israelite, of the seed of Abraham, of the tribe of Benjamin." If God has rejected His people, why was Paul, an Israelite, a

71

believer in Jesus? Paul's conversion proves that God is not through with the Jewish people. Not only was he Jewish; he was a Jew with a pure pedigree. Paul was a Jew not by proselytism (a proselyte is a Gentile convert to Judaism), but by blood line. As a physical descendant of Abraham, Paul was born a Jew.

In addition to identifying himself as "of the seed of Abraham," the apostle described himself as "of the tribe of Benjamin." Apparently Paul was concerned that people know his tribal heritage, for in Philippians 3:5 he again mentioned that he was a Benjamite. Why was this information important? After the death of Solomon the united kingdom of Israel divided. Ten tribes noted for their idolatry and apostasy broke off and formed the northern kingdom of Israel. The only tribe that remained faithful to Judah in the southern kingdom was Benjamin. As a result the tribe of Benjamin was highly respected. Many esteemed Jews were Benjamites, such as King Saul, his son Jonathan, Esther, and Mordecai.

To be from the tribe of Benjamin was a great honor in the eyes of the Jewish people. The fact that Paul was a Benjamite strengthened his argument that God wasn't finished with Israel. How could God have rejected His people when Paul, a pure Jew from an honored tribe, was a believer in Jesus? Paul was a Jew's Jew and his conversion was ample proof that God had not canceled His promises of salvation to Israel.

The apostle's conversion indicated that God isn't through with the nation of Israel in spite of her unbelief. If ever there was a Jewish candidate to be rejected by God for his persecution of Christ, it was Paul. He described his preconversion behavior and ultimate salvation as follows:

> Who was before a blasphemer, and a persecutor, and injurious: but I obtained mercy, because I did it ignorantly in unbelief. And the grace of our Lord was exceeding abundant with faith and love which is in

Christ Jesus. This is a faithful saying, and worthy of all acceptation, that Christ Jesus came into the world to save sinners; of whom I am chief. Howbeit for this cause I obtained mercy, that in me first Jesus Christ might shew forth all longsuffering, for a pattern to them which should hereafter believe on him to life everlasting (1 Timothy 1:13-16).

Paul was a living illustration of God's mercy and patience in saving Christ-rejecting sinners. If God had totally rejected Israel because they rejected Him, He would not have saved the greatest rejecter of them all. Paul's point in presenting himself as a saved Israelite was to make this statement: If God saved the greatest Christ-rejecting Jew, certainly He is not through saving other Jewish Christ-rejecters!

THE CHOSEN REMNANT - ROMANS 11:2-6

Paul offered the chosen remnant as the second line of proof in his argument that God has not rejected Israel. In Romans 9 Paul introduced the concept of the remnant as the elect minority of Jewish people who trust God as their father Abraham did. In Romans 11 Paul once again mentioned this chosen remnant as proof of God's faithfulness to Israel. The apostle wrote, "God hath not cast away his people which he foreknew" (11:2).

Many people assume that the word *foreknew* means "knew beforehand," but the word actually suggests a predetermined and preplanned love relationship. The word *know* is often used in Scripture to refer to setting one's love upon another. For example when God said to Israel, "You only have I known of all the families of the earth" (Amos 3:2), He meant, "You are the only family on the face of the earth that I have set my heart upon." Therefore, for God to foreknow His people is to choose them to be the special objects of His love. Paul's

point was that God has not broken His promises and cut off the
nation He chose to be His special people.

To illustrate the fact that God will never cast away His
people, regardless of their disobedience, Paul cited a national
crisis in Elijah's day:

> Wot ye not what the scripture saith of [Elijah]? how he
> maketh intercession to God against Israel, saying, Lord,
> they have killed thy prophets, and digged down thine
> altars; and I am left alone, and they seek my life. But
> what saith the answer of God unto Him? I have re-
> served to myself seven thousand men, who have not
> bowed the knee to the image of Baal (Romans 11:2-4).

Elijah, a great Hebrew prophet, was God's spokesman to
Israel in one of the nation's darkest hours, when the Jewish
people were deeply involved in idolatry. Led by King Ahab
and his wicked pagan wife Jezebel, the nation had rejected the
Lord and instituted the worship of Baal as the official religion
of Israel. Frustrated over Israel's apostasy, Elijah asked God to
reject His people in judgment (1 Kings 19:10,14).

God responded to the prophet by having him witness a
powerful wind, an earthquake, and a fire. Each of these
natural phenomena is well known for its capacity to kill men.
Yet the Biblical record reveals that God was not present in
these natural catastrophes. He was present, however, in a still
small voice (1 Kings 19:11-12).

This unusual incident indicates that while Elijah desired
God to destroy Israel in judgment, God's heart was tender
toward them. With a still small voice God was reaching out to
Israel with His grace. Elijah thought that he was the only one
who had remained true to God, but God revealed to him that a
remnant of seven thousand Jewish men had remained faithful
(1 Kings 19:18). While the nation as a whole was unbelieving,
God refused to destroy Israel because of the believing remnant.

What was true in Elijah's day was also true in Paul's day. The apostle wrote, "Even so then at this present time also there is a remnant according to the election of grace" (Romans 11:5). While national Israel rejected Jesus as Messiah, the first-century church included many Hebrew Christians. Paul identified these believers as the "remnant according to the election of grace." His point was that just as the chosen remnant in Elijah's day kept God from casting off Israel, the remnant in Paul's day was accomplishing the same result. The chosen remnant's presence proved that God had not rejected the nation of Israel.

The fact that there have been Jewish believers in every generation throughout the church age indicates that God has not permanently cast away His people. When I accepted the Lord, I thought I was the only Jewish person in the whole world who had ever become a Christian. The Gentile believers I knew did little to correct my thinking. I was the first Hebrew Christian most of them had ever met. They tended to place me on exhibit like a one-of-a-kind species.

My well-meaning Gentile brethren should have known that God always reserves for Himself a remnant of Jewish believers. His tender, still small voice is ever reaching out to save Jews. And the remnant always respond to His grace. Paul wrote, "If by grace, then is it no more of works: otherwise grace is no more grace. But if it be of works, then it is no more grace: otherwise work is no more work" (Romans 11:6). Unlike the majority of Israelites who try to merit God's favor by their good works, the remnant trust Christ to save them by His grace. They understand that grace stands alone, apart from good works. Grace and works are mutually exclusive.

THE CONDITION OF ISRAEL - ROMANS 11:7-10

The third line of evidence in Paul's argument that God has not rejected Israel is the condition of the Hebrew people. In

Romans 11:7 Paul stated the spiritual condition of the majority of Israel: "Israel hath not obtained that which he seeketh for; but the election hath obtained it, and the rest were blinded." The apostle was declaring that the mass of natural Israel is in a state of spiritual insensitivity.

The word that is translated "blinded" *(pōroō)* is related to the Greek word *porosis,* which is similar to our English word "paralysis." *Pōroō* means "to cover with a thick skin, to harden by covering with a callous."[1] Calloused skin is insensitive. It has lost its feeling as in paralysis. The Jewish people were insensitive to the gospel because God had hardened them. As a result of Israel's hardness, God judicially hardened them further so that they could not believe the truth about Christ.

While judicial hardness may at first glance seem unfair, we must realize that God hardened Israel only after they hardened themselves. The concept of judicial hardness was not new to Paul's readers. The Hebrew Scriptures refer to it quite often. Paul referred to the writings of Moses and David to confirm that a chosen remnant has always existed within a God-hardened nation. Quoting Deuteronomy 29:4 and Psalm 69:22-23 the apostle wrote:

> (According as it is written, God hath given them the spirit of slumber, eyes that they should not see, and ears that they should not hear;) unto this day. And David saith, Let their table be made a snare, and a trap, and a stumblingblock, and a recompense unto them: Let their eyes be darkened, that they may not see, and bow down their back alway" (Romans 11:8-10).

Paul's purpose in quoting these Hebrew prophets was to prove that Israel's rejection of Jesus did not result in God's permanently setting the nation aside. Their rejection of Messiah was the consummation of their blindness and hardness of heart, and not the cause of it. The apostle John interpreted Israel's rejection of Christ as a direct result of the hardening of God. John wrote:

> Though he had done so many miracles before them, yet they believed not on him: That the saying of [Isaiah] the prophet might be fulfilled, which he spake, Lord, who hath believed our report? and to whom hath the arm of the Lord been revealed? Therefore they could not believe, because that [Isaiah] said again, He hath blinded their eyes, and hardened their heart; that they should not see with their eyes, nor understand with their heart, and be converted, and I should heal them (John 12:37-40).

Israel's long history reveals that because they did not want to believe God's truth down through the ages, God hardened them to the point that when the Truth (Jesus Christ) finally stood in their midst, they could not recognize Him for who He was. The Hebrew prophets confirmed that the majority of Israelites have always been disobedient and rebellious to God's Word. Since unbelief on the part of the majority never canceled God's promises to Israel before, their rejection of Messiah did not cancel the promises either.

Has God cast away His people? How could anyone ever think such a thought when the conversion of Paul, the chosen remnant, and the condition of Israel prove otherwise?

---

1. Fritz Rienecker and Cleon Rogers, *Linguistic Key to the Greek New Testament* (Grand Rapids: Zondervan, 1980) 372.

Chapter 8

WHY DID ISRAEL STUMBLE?

Romans 11:11-15

W hen Frederick the Great, king of Prussia, asked his chaplain to give him the strongest evidence for the Christian faith, his chaplain's reply was "The Jew!"[1] Long after other great civilizations have expired, the Jewish people stand as a testimony to the trustworthiness of God's Word.

Throughout Biblical history God promised the Hebrew nation that He would preserve them forever. Yet in Paul's day there was a growing concern that God had rejected Israel because of her rejection of Jesus as Messiah. Since the church was predominantly Gentile, it seemed that God had set Israel aside while He established His church. Addressing this concern in Romans 11:11-15, the apostle Paul explained that Israel's unbelief had not frustrated God's promises to Israel; instead their unbelief had resulted in the fulfillment of God's redemptive plan for mankind.

Paul began this passage with a penetrating question: "Have they stumbled that they should fall?" (11:11) Paul had previously asserted that Israel's rejection of Jesus was like a person stumbling (11:9). Now he was asking why they stumbled. Did they stumble beyond recovery? Did Israel stumble with such a crash that they would never be able to get up again? What was God's purpose in allowing Israel to stumble? Did He intend to remove the nation from the place of blessing permanently? The answer was given immediately:

"God forbid" (11:11). Israel has been set aside only temporarily during the church age.

The issue that the apostle raised is this: If Israel's rejection
of Christ did not result in God's permanent rejection of them,
why did God permit such widespread Jewish unbelief? What
divine purposes could be served by the stumbling of Israel? In
response to his own question, Paul first defined God's sovereign purposes and then demonstrated how they were being
fulfilled.

GOD'S SOVEREIGN PURPOSES DECLARED
ROMANS 11:11-12

God's sovereign purposes include the salvation of the
Gentiles, the salvation of Israel, and blessings for the world.

The Salvation of Gentiles

Paul wrote, "Through their fall salvation is come unto the
Gentiles" (11:11). When the Jewish people turned away from
the message of Christ, God turned the gospel away from them
and sent it to the Gentile world. Early proclaimers of the gospel were so consumed with proclaiming Christ that when
their message was not received by the Jewish community,
they turned to the Gentiles (Acts 13:46-48; 18:6).

Jesus predicted that Israel's rejection of Him as Messiah
would result in the salvation of the Gentiles. He said, "Therefore say I unto you, The kingdom of God shall be taken from
you, and given to a nation bringing forth the fruits thereof"
(Matthew 21:43). On the day of Pentecost when the church
was born, God temporarily set Israel aside. His program
turned to calling out a remnant of Jews and a large number of
Gentiles to form His body, the church.

Those who believe that God is finished with Israel fail to
comprehend that for two thousand years God has used their
sin to reach Gentiles and to build Christ's church. The

predominately Gentile church of today gives evidence of
God's sovereignty in fulfilling His purposes through the
disobedience of Israel.

The Salvation of Israel

God did not temporarily set Israel aside to abandon them,
but rather to save them. Paul wrote, "Through their fall
salvation is come unto the Gentiles, for to provoke them to
jealousy" (11:11). The conversion of Gentiles during the
church age is designed to stir the Jewish people to jealousy so
that they will desire what Gentile Christians have and consequently turn to the Lord.

A day is coming in which the Hebrew nation will finally
realize that Gentiles are enjoying the blessings of the salvation
Israel rejected. This realization will provoke Israel to a jealousy that will result in their embracing Jesus as Messiah
(11:26).

Blessings for the World

God will sovereignly use the fall of Israel to bless the
world. Paul wrote, "If the fall of them be the riches of the
world, and the diminishing of them the riches of the Gentiles;
how much more their fulness?" (11:12) If Israel's loss is the
gain of the Gentiles, what riches are in store for the whole
world when God restores the Jewish nation to her position of
privilege?

The riches Paul was referring to are the blessings the
world will experience during the millennial kingdom after
the Jewish nation turns to Christ (Romans 11:26). At that time
the curse will be lifted, paradise will be regained, the animal
kingdom will be at peace, the Lord will reign out of Jerusalem,
the Old Testament saints will be resurrected, the shekinah
glory will once again fill the temple, Satan will be bound,
Israel and the church will reign with Christ, and peace, joy,
and righteousness will prevail (Isaiah 11; Revelation 20–22).

GOD'S SOVEREIGN PURPOSES DEMONSTRATED
ROMANS 11:13-15

Even though the church at Rome was predominately Gentile and Paul was the apostle to the Gentiles, he devoted much of his Epistle to the welfare of Israel. Some members of the church apparently saw this as an inconsistency in the apostle's ministry. However, Paul's ardent interest in Israel was consistent with his apostleship to the Gentiles.

He explained his mission to the Gentiles by writing, "I speak to you Gentiles, inasmuch as I am the apostle of the Gentiles, I magnify mine office" (Romans 11:13). Throughout his ministry Paul often affirmed the fact that God had called him to be the apostle to the Gentiles (Galatians 1:15-16; Ephesians 3:8; 1 Timothy 2:7; 2 Timothy 4:17). He considered this office a glorious calling since it was in harmony with God's plan to bless the world.

Paul saw the salvation of Gentiles as the means by which Jewish people would see their need for Jesus Christ. The apostle defended his interest in Israel when he wrote, "If by any means I may provoke to emulation them which are my flesh, and might save some of them" (Romans 11:14). Some Jews would be stirred to jealousy by observing the spiritual dynamics in the lives of Gentile Christians. The sparkling testimonies of godly Gentile believers would incite Jewish people to want the salvation that produced such changed lives.

The apostle's approach to Jewish evangelism gives us great insight into how to reach Jewish people with the gospel. During the church age God's primary method for bringing Jewish people to Christ is through godly Gentile Christians. From a human perspective, I came to Christ because a Gentile believer's life was spiritually attractive. When I realized that his life was characterized by peace, joy, satisfaction, purpose, and love, I was moved to jealousy. I wanted what he had. The reality of Christ in his life revealed the emptiness of my life.

In light of Paul's method of reaching Jewish people for the Lord, it would appear that Gentile believers make the most effective witnesses. While Hebrew Christians may be more adept at relating to their kinsmen, the transformed character of a Gentile believer makes the greatest impression on an unsaved Jew. While most Jewish people look on Hebrew Christians with suspicion, they are intrigued by the testimonies of Gentiles who have come to embrace a Jewish Messiah revealed in a Jewish book.

The best way for Gentile Christians to reach out to Jewish people is to live spiritually attractive lives before them. The unsaved Jewish community should perceive Gentile believers as possessing a quality of life worth emulating. When Gentile believers lead spiritually shallow lives, they harm the cause of Christ. Instead of presenting a vibrant Christianity that is genuinely attractive, they present a religion of hypocrisy. Far from provoking Jewish people to jealousy, inconsistent living leads them away from the gospel. They conclude, "Why should I become a Christian when my behavior is better than that of the Christians I know?"

While Paul had a deep burden for the salvation of his fellow Jews (Romans 9:3; 10:1), his concern for Jewish evangelism went beyond personal feelings. He summed up his great interest in Jewish evangelism when he wrote, "If the casting away of them be the reconciling of the world, what shall the receiving of them be, but life from the dead?" (11:15). Paul's interest in the salvation of Jewish people was intense since the salvation of Israel will result in the world being blessed during the millennial kingdom.

Every Christian should be interested in Jewish evangelism because it is tied to God's future redemptive plan. The most effective way to reach out to Jewish people with the gospel is to live a godly life before them. In addition to a verbal witness, the testimony of a spiritually attractive lifestyle speaks volumes to Jewish people. Do you lead the kind of Christian life that can provoke them to jealousy?

---

1. John Philips, *Exploring the World of the Jew* (Neptune, NJ: Loizeaux, 1993) 9.

Chapter 9

THE RESTORATION OF ISRAEL

Romans 11:16-29

Every Gentile Christian should have a keen interest in the future of the Jewish people. Without a firm belief in a future plan for Israel, a Gentile can open himself up to pride and arrogance toward the Jew. To believe that God has permanently cast away the Hebrew nation can lead to an attitude of spiritual superiority over Jewish people. However, to believe in Israel's future restoration to the place of divine privilege and blessing leads to a proper self-evaluation and understanding of God's grace.

In Romans 11:16-29 Paul addressed Gentiles in the church at Rome who looked down on Israel because of her unbelief. He warned them about the grave danger of pride and arrogance toward Israel. To indicate the glorious future of Israel, Paul stated the principle of Israel's restoration, the possibility of her restoration, and the promise of her restoration.

THE PRINCIPLE OF ISRAEL'S RESTORATION
ROMANS 11:16-22

Paul began by presenting two analogies that illustrate the principle of Israel's restoration. He wrote, "If the firstfruit be holy, the lump is also holy: and if the root be holy, so are the branches" (11:16). The analogy of the dough is a reference to the Mosaic law in Numbers 15:18-21. The law required that each time dough was prepared for baking bread, a little piece of the dough was to be given to the Lord—that is, to the priest. This symbolic act indicated that the whole lump belonged to God. The analogy of the tree is a matter of common sense. If the root of a tree is consecrated ("holy") to God, then the branches that come from that tree are also set apart for Him.

Both of these analogies illustrate the principle of God's restoring Israel to her place of privilege. The first piece of dough and the root of the tree represent the origin of Israel in the person of Abraham. The tree, which stems from the root, represents the place of privilege and blessing stemming from the unconditional covenant made with Abraham (Genesis 12:1-3). The lump and the branches refer to the Jewish people.

Paul was making the point that since Israel is rooted in the covenant promises made to Abraham, the nation is set apart for God. In other words, because Abraham was set apart for God, all the Jewish people who come out from his loins are set apart as well. Paul was using the term "holy" in the sense of being set apart for God's use, rather than in the sense of being morally holy. If Israel has been set apart for God's use, her stumbling must be temporary and her restoration inevitable.

However, in the process of temporarily setting Israel aside, other branches were grafted in. Paul wrote, "Some of the branches [were] broken off, and thou, being a wild olive tree, wert graffed in among them, and with them partakest of the root and fatness of the olive tree" (Romans 11:17). When God set Israel aside, He cut off unbelieving Jewish branches from the tree. Then He took branches from a wild olive tree (Gentile believers) and grafted them into the cultivated tree. Together with Jewish believing branches, Gentile branches can now enjoy the spiritual blessings that come from the covenant made with Abraham. However, this grafting in does not warrant an attitude of boastfulness on the part of the Gentile branches.

In the church age Gentiles who become Christians have

spiritual privileges that Jewish unbelievers do not have, but Gentile branches need to beware of religious pride. Because they are in the place of blessing where the broken-off branches used to be, the Gentiles can easily think of themselves as better than the Jews.

Warning against this natural tendency toward pride, Paul wrote, "Boast not against the branches. But if thou boast, thou bearest not the root, but the root thee" (Romans 11:18). The apostle was telling Gentile believers not to look down on Jewish people who have rejected Christ. If the Gentile Christians do exalt themselves, they should remember that they aren't the source of blessing. Abraham, the Jewish root, is the source of the blessings that Gentile believers experience. As Jesus declared, "Salvation is of the Jews" (John 4:22). Gentile believers are linked to Abraham in the sense that the patriarch is "the father of all them that believe" (Romans 4:11).

Gentile branches might also believe that God cut the Jewish branches off from the tree of blessing because Gentile believers were more deserving. The apostle Paul anticipated such a Gentile claim to superiority over unbelieving Jews by writing, "Thou wilt say then, The branches were broken off, that I might be graffed in" (Romans 11:19).

When the Gentile church considers itself more deserving of salvation than Jewish people who have rejected Christ, she displays an intolerable arrogance. Ironically, this attitude is similar to the thinking of Israel in Old Testament days. The ancient Jew was often bigoted and proud and sometimes thought that God could only establish a relationship with him—and not with a Gentile. Paul captured this haughty Jewish spirit when he described the attitude of superiority over Gentiles with these words: "[Thou] art confident that thou thyself art a guide of the blind, a light of them which are in darkness, An instructor of the foolish, a teacher of babes, which hast the form of knowledge and of the truth in the law" (Romans 2:19-20).

When Gentile Christendom exhibited a similar attitude, a rebuke from the apostle was warranted. Therefore Paul wrote, "Because of unbelief they were broken off, and thou standest by faith. Be not highminded, but fear: For if God spared not the natural branches, take heed lest he also spare not thee" (Romans 11:20-21). In addition to rebuking proud Gentiles, Paul was explaining why the Jewish branches were cut off and exhorting the Gentiles to fear God.

The reason unbelieving Jewish branches were cut off from the place of blessing had nothing to do with Jewish inferiority to Gentiles. The real reason was related to the issue of faith. The Jewish branches were cut off because of their unbelief and the Gentile branches were grafted in because of their faith in Christ. Why then should Gentile branches fear? If God did not spare the original people of the covenant because of their unbelief, He certainly will not spare Gentiles if they do not believe. "Why should God have any more regard for a faithless Gentile Christianity than for a faithless Judaism?"[1]

Would God ever cut unbelieving Gentiles off as He cut off unbelieving Jews? Paul answered this question by writing, "Behold therefore the goodness and severity of God: on them which fell, severity; but toward thee, goodness, if thou continue in his goodness: otherwise thou also shalt be cut off" (Romans 11:22). Just as the olive tree had unbelieving Jews who were cut off, so the professing church certainly has unbelieving Gentiles who will be cut off. Paul wasn't suggesting that true believers will be lost, since he had already established the security of the believer in Romans 8. However, much of what is called Christendom is the liberal apostate church that claims to be Christian but denies the deity of Christ, attacks the Bible, and scorns the gospel! Just as all Israel is not Israel, so all Christendom is not the church (Romans 9:6).

Gentiles who turn from the goodness of God will be cut off from the place of blessing. These unbelieving branches are

Gentiles who never experience salvation, but by their associa-
tion and identification with true believers experience some of
the blessings God gives to His church (see 1 Corinthians 7:14).
A day is coming when the false Gentile church will be cut off
from the place of blessing. After the rapture of the church, the
false church will continue into the tribulation period until she
is cut off by the antichrist (Revelation 17).

If it is possible for the false Gentile church to be cut off
because of her unbelief, it must also be possible for Israel to be
grafted back in if she should come to believe the gospel.

THE POSSIBILITY OF ISRAEL'S RESTORATION
ROMANS 11:23-24

Can God restore Israel? The answer is yes! Therefore Paul
continued writing to the Gentile branches, "They also, if they
abide not still in unbelief, shall be graffed in: for God is able
to graff them in again" (11:23). Without specifically stating
that Israel will turn to Christ, the apostle declared that if they
ever did believe the gospel, God is able and willing to graft
them back into the tree.

In addition to being possible, restoration would not be
difficult for God. Paul wrote, "If thou wert cut out of the olive
tree which is wild by nature, and wert graffed contrary to
nature into a good olive tree: how much more shall these,
which be the natural branches, be graffed into their own olive
tree?" (11:24) Some insight on the grafting procedure helps us
to understand this verse:

> The olive, in its natural wild state, bears no berries, or
> but few, and these small and destitute of oil.
> ...The olive...is wild by nature, and it must be
> grafted by the *good* before it will bear fruit; but here the
> Apostle speaks of grafting the wild into the good, not
> the good *upon* the wild.

...observe, he says expressly that this is *contrary* to nature, as it really is. I have made particular inquiries on this point, and find that in the *kingdom of nature* generally, certainly in the case of the olive, the process referred to by the Apostle never succeeds. Graft the good upon the wild, and, as the Arabs say, it will *conquer* the wild; but you cannot reverse the process with success.—If you insert a *wild* graft into a good tree, *it will conquer the good*. It is only in the *kingdom of grace* that a process thus contrary to nature can be successful; and it is this circumstance which the Apostle has seized upon, and with admirable tact, to magnify the mercy shown to the Gentiles by grafting them, a wild race, *contrary to the nature* of such operations, into the good olive-tree.[2]

Gentiles should never glory over the unbelieving Jews' present estate. If God can do such an unnatural thing as graft Gentiles into a good tree, how much more easily He could graft the natural branches into their own olive tree! In other words, if God could take idolatrous pagans and bring them to the Jewish religion, He could more easily lead straying Jews back to their own original religion.

A Hebrew Christian may be considered a novelty today, but there is nothing more natural and normal than for a Jew to believe in Jesus. It is abnormal for a Jewish person *not* to believe in Jesus as Messiah. What is remarkable is that throughout the dark history of paganism so many Gentiles have placed their faith in Jesus Christ.

The future restoration of Israel depends upon faith. Today unbelief prevents Jews from being grafted into their own olive tree. However, both the principle and the possibility of restoration indicate a glorious future for the Hebrew nation.

A number of years ago Dr. William Culbertson of Moody Bible Institute wrote a letter to David Ben-Gurion, the first prime minister of Israel. After thanking Mr. Ben-Gurion for meeting with him during his stay in Israel, Dr. Culbertson wrote these words:

> Our visit to Israel was very wonderful. I continue to marvel at the initiative, the industry and the utter devotion of the people to the work of rebuilding Israel. It is a source of inspiration indeed. Some of us, of course, believe that this could well be the prelude to what the Old Testament prophets predicted. You manifested such a complete grasp of the religious side of the matter that I am sure you know some of us do believe in a personal Messiah and that there are days of great glory awaiting your nation.[3]

David Ben-Gurion isn't the only one in history who had to be told of the glorious future awaiting the Jewish people. The predominately Gentile church at Rome also lacked understanding of God's plan to save and restore Israel to the place of privileged blessing. Therefore, after instructing the church on the possibility of restoration, Paul informed them of the promise of Israel's restoration.

THE PROMISE OF ISRAEL'S RESTORATION
ROMANS 11:25-29

The purpose of the apostle's instruction was to correct the arrogant attitude of Gentiles who looked down on Israel's spiritual blindness. Focusing on this blindness, Paul answered four key questions concerning Israel's coming restoration.

1. When Will Israel's Blindness End?

Paul wrote, "For I would not, brethren, that ye should be ignorant of this mystery, lest ye should be wise in your own conceits; that blindness in part is happened to Israel, until the fulness of the Gentiles be come in" (Romans 11:25). To deliver the predominately Gentile church at Rome from self-exaltation, Paul informed them that Israel's blindness will come to an end. He called this fact a "mystery." In the Bible a mystery is not something that is difficult to understand, uncanny, or mysterious. A Biblical mystery is truth previously hidden in the mind of God but now revealed by Him for the first time (Ephesians 3:1-5). In essence a mystery is newly revealed information.

What was this new information regarding Israel's hardness toward God? The revelation certainly was not that Israel was partially hardened. It was a well-known Biblical truth that only a remnant of Jewish people in each generation would believe in the Lord. The Hebrew Scriptures clearly reveal that the majority of Israel had historically been in rebellion toward God (see 1 Kings 19:18 and Isaiah 1).

It was well known that blindness in part had happened to Israel, but it was not known how long that blindness would last. The length of the blindness was the mystery that had been hidden in the heart of God. He had chosen not to reveal this information until He made it known through Paul in Romans 11:25. Paul taught that the nation of Israel would remain blind to the truth of the gospel "until the fulness of the Gentiles be come in." In other words, Israel will be blind until the last Gentile in the church age has been brought to Christ.

"The fulness of the Gentiles" describes the present age, during which God is saving many Gentiles. In Acts 15:14 James said, "Simeon hath declared how God at the first did visit the Gentiles, to take out of them a people for his name." While individual Jews (the remnant) are being saved today, the present age is primarily a time when God is visiting the Gentiles. The nation of Israel will remain hardened to the gospel until the church is raptured at the close of this age. Then, during the seven-year tribulation period, God will again focus His attention on Israel in order to bring her to Himself and to restore her to a place of blessing.

2. Who Will End Israel's Blindness?

Having established the fact that Israel's blindness will end when the church age ends, Paul then revealed that the Lord Jesus Christ, at His return, will put an end to Israel's blindness. The apostle wrote, "And so all Israel shall be saved: as it is written, There shall come out of [Zion] the Deliverer, and shall turn away ungodliness from Jacob" (Romans 11:26).

During the tribulation period Satan will attempt to destroy Israel (Revelation 12). Zechariah announced that two-thirds of the Jewish population will die during this time (Zechariah 13:8). The horrors of the tribulation will include Satanic persecution, natural catastrophes, and unprecedented demonic activity. Jeremiah referred to this period as "the time of Jacob's trouble" (Jeremiah 30:7). Jesus declared that the great tribulation will be a time of unparalleled devastation. He said, "For then shall be great tribulation, such as was not since the beginning of the world to this time, no, nor ever shall be" (Matthew 24:21).

While the Jewish population will be dramatically reduced during the tribulation period, God will protect and preserve a remnant. The prophet Zechariah declared that the remaining one-third of the Jewish people will go through a period of intense suffering that will result in their turning to the Lord. Zechariah 13:9 records the words of the Lord: "And I will bring the third part through the fire, and will refine them as silver is refined, and will try them as gold is tried: they shall call on my name, and I will hear them: I will say, It is my people: and they shall say, The Lord is my God."

The surviving remnant of Jewish people alive at the end of the tribulation will constitute the entire nation of Israel. Therefore Paul referred to both the remnant and the nation when he wrote, "And so all Israel shall be saved." This statement certainly doesn't mean that every Jew who has ever lived will be saved; it means that all the Jews who are alive when Christ returns will be saved.

During the tribulation period the nation of Israel will acknowledge and accept Jesus as Messiah. After the nation has been purged of unbelieving Jewish rebels (Ezekiel 20:33-38), Christ will remove the blindness of Israel and the nation will finally recognize their Messiah. Zechariah described Israel's future repentance when Messiah comes:

> And I will pour upon the house of David, and upon the inhabitants of Jerusalem, the spirit of grace and of supplications: and they shall look upon me whom they have pierced, and they shall mourn for him, as one mourneth for his only son, and shall be in bitterness for him, as one that is in bitterness for his firstborn (Zechariah 12:10).

3. Why Will Israel's Blindness Be Removed?

Why will Christ "turn away ungodliness from Jacob"? Why will the Lord bring Israel to Himself? The answer is given in Romans 11:27: "For this is my covenant unto them, when I shall take away their sins." The apostle was quoting from Isaiah 59:21, which associates the coming of Messiah with the new covenant. The prophet Jeremiah foretold that the new covenant which God would make with Israel would provide forgiveness of their sins (Jeremiah 31:31-34). The reason Christ will lift Israel's blindness is to fulfill His Word to bring Israel under the new covenant.

Arriving at Romans 11:27, Paul had gone full circle with the argument that began in Romans 9:6. He had dealt with the concern over God's faithfulness in keeping His promise of salvation to Israel. The apostle had affirmed that at the return of Christ all Israel will be saved; God will remain true to His Word to forgive the sins of repentant Israel. Paul had vindicated God's name. He had brilliantly defended the righteousness of God in His dealings with Israel. But one more issue remained to be settled by the apostle: his readers had a fourth key question about the blindness of Israel. Paul had answered the question before, but the answer needed reinforcing.

4. What Was the Purpose of Israel's Blindness?

In Romans 11:11-15 Paul had explained God's purposes in allowing Israel to stumble. Now the apostle summed up his explanation in Romans 11:28: "As concerning the gospel, they are enemies for your sakes: but as touching the election, they are beloved for the fathers' sakes."

Let the Gentile church understand that God has withheld the gospel from Israel in order to offer it to Gentiles. However, Israel remains the elect nation, beloved by God because of His promises made to Abraham, Isaac, and Jacob. Today Israel is an enemy of the gospel, but in the future restoration God will treat Israelites as friends.

When the Lord promised the Jewish patriarchs that He would make them a blessed nation, His promise was irrevocable. He who called Israel into existence, bestowed numerous gifts upon her, and promised her future glory will fulfill His Word. God's purposes for Israel will be accomplished in spite of her present blindness. How can we be so certain? Because Romans 11:29 says, "The gifts and calling of God are without repentance."

Jewish blindness to the gospel should never be a cause for Gentile self-exaltation. Israel's unbelief has resulted in the salvation of countless Gentiles. Instead of responding in pride, the Gentile church should be humbled by the mercy God has shown to them.

1. Stifler, *Romans,* 153.
2. Thomson, William M., *The Land and the Book* (Grand Rapids: Baker, 1954) 53.
3. Warren W. Wiersbe, *William Culbertson, A Man of God* (Chicago: Moody Press, 1974) 128.

CONCLUSION

Chapter 10

THE MERCIES OF GOD

Romans 11:30–12:1

A friend and I were once discussing the difference between God's program for Israel and His program for the church. Toward the end of our conversation my friend asked, "Why does God have different programs for these two groups of people?" I answered his question with one word: "Mercy." God's compassion and kindness lie behind His dealings with Israel and His dealings with the church. He has established both Israel and the church in order to display His mercy to Jews and Gentiles who believe in Him. Out of mercy to Gentiles God planned a time of blindness for Israel; out of mercy to Israel He planned the church age when Gentiles would proclaim the gospel to Jews.

The apostle Paul closed his defense of the righteousness of God's dealings with Israel by focusing on the concept of God's mercy. His purpose in emphasizing mercy was to humble some proud Gentiles who considered themselves spiritually superior to unbelieving Jews. To combat Gentile arrogance, the apostle informed the church at Rome that God's program for salvation stems from His mercy rather than from anything inherently good in man. In Romans 11:30–12:1 Paul magnified God's kindness toward Jews and Gentiles by presenting three important truths about God's mercy: (1) God's mercy has been revealed; (2) God's mercy results in praise; and (3) God's mercy demands a response.

GOD'S MERCY HAS BEEN REVEALED - ROMANS 11:30-32

First Paul faced Gentiles with the fact that their salvation is based on God's mercy. He wrote, "Ye in times past have not believed God, yet have now obtained mercy through their unbelief" (11:30). Paul contrasted Gentiles (identified as "ye") and Jews (identified as "their"). Gentiles were once unbelieving rebels, but God in mercy offered them salvation when Israel rejected Jesus as Messiah.

God's mercy is the only reason there are more Gentile Christians than Jewish Christians during the church age. The statistics have nothing to do with spiritual inclination. While much of the Bible is devoted to recording Israel's hardness and unbelief, Gentile wickedness is also honestly exposed. The New Testament reveals an ugly picture of Gentile behavior in the ancient world. Paul characterized the non-Christian Gentile as walking in the vanity of his mind, darkened in understanding, spiritually ignorant and blind, morally calloused, sensual, and impure (Ephesians 4:17-19). The apostle presented the pagan world as suppressing God's truths and indulging in vile and unnatural affections:

> Filled with all unrighteousness, fornication, wickedness, covetousness, maliciousness; full of envy, murder, debate, deceit, malignity; whisperers, Backbiters, haters of God, despiteful, proud, boasters, inventors of evil things, disobedient to parents, Without understanding, covenantbreakers, without natural affection, implacable, unmerciful (Romans 1:29-31).

One of the most amazing concepts, often overlooked by evangelical Christians, is not that Israel will one day be restored, but that so many pagan Gentiles have come to Christ for salvation. The cure for a Gentile's pride is for him to realize that God permitted the Gentiles to sink to the depths of sin before He mercifully reached out to them in forming His church. Their salvation is purely a product of God's mercy to a disobedient people.

But Gentiles are not the only recipients of God's mercy. God has also extended His mercy to Jewish people. Paul continued, "Even so have these [Jews] also now not believed, that through your mercy they also may obtain mercy" (Romans 11:31).

When Gentile Christians take the gospel to Jewish people, the Gentiles' kindness gives Jews the opportunity to experience God's mercy. In other words, by the mercy of the Gentiles, Jews too can find God's mercy. This truth should stimulate Jewish evangelism. Gentile believers are the primary instruments God uses to proclaim the gospel to Jewish people. God's evangelistic pattern is to reveal His mercy to undeserving Jewish sinners through undeserving Gentile sinners who have been mercifully saved.

God's ultimate plan is to reveal His mercy to both unbelieving Jews and Gentiles as they believe the gospel. Paul wrote, "For God hath concluded them all in unbelief, that he might have mercy upon all" (Romans 11:32). In the Greek text this verse reveals the fact that all mankind has been imprisoned in disobedience so that God can show mercy to those who turn to Him. Although everyone deserves eternal judgment, God does not send everyone to Hell. Instead He locks up all in sin so that He can reveal how merciful He is to all who trust Him.

GOD'S MERCY RESULTS IN PRAISE - ROMANS 11:33-36

After explaining that God has used the sin of Israel to reveal His mercy to Gentiles and Jews, the apostle broke into a doxology. He wrote:

O the depth of the riches both of the wisdom and

> knowledge of God! how unsearchable are his judg-
> ments, and his ways past finding out! For who hath
> known the mind of the Lord? or who hath been his
> counsellor? Or who hath first given to him, and it
> shall be recompensed unto him again? (Romans 11:33-
> 35).

Only the mind of God could formulate a plan of salvation that would redeem ruined Jews and Gentiles! Only the mind of God could take the fall of Israel and turn it into salvation for Gentiles, salvation for Jews, salvation for the nation of Israel, and blessings for the entire world! Only the mind of God could plan to accomplish this in a way that is consistent with the Old Testament, does not violate His righteousness, and exalts His mercy.

The result of God's mercy is praise—praise for His mind, wisdom, knowledge, decisions, and ways. These attributes are so deep and rich that they are unsearchable and untrace-able. God is so great that our minds cannot even grasp the fullness of His greatness. No one knows what is on God's mind unless He reveals it. No one counsels God. No one does anything for God that makes Him a debtor. No wonder Paul concluded his doxology with these words: "For of him, and through him, and to him, are all things: to whom be glory for ever. Amen" (Romans 11:36).

How humbling it must have been for the proud Gentile Christians at Rome to hear that God must be praised for their salvation. They did not deserve the credit themselves. God's mercy is responsible for salvation. God created the plan of salvation; He has sustained the plan; and He will bring the plan to completion for the purpose of bringing glory to Himself.

Romans 11:36 is the highest point of this Epistle. It took Paul eleven chapters to build up to this verse and the state-ment demands a response from every redeemed person.

GOD'S MERCY DEMANDS A RESPONSE - ROMANS 12:1

God has mercifully given salvation to previously hostile Jews and Gentiles. What should our response be? Paul wrote that there is only one reasonable response: "I beseech you therefore, brethren, by the mercies of God, that ye present your bodies a living sacrifice, holy, acceptable unto God, which is your reasonable service" (Romans 12:1). Based on God's magnificent mercies revealed throughout this letter to the Romans, Paul's plea was for the brethren to give God their bodies. Because God has been so kind to us, we are urged to respond by presenting ourselves to Him.

In Old Testament times a Hebrew worshiper would present an unblemished animal sacrifice to God as an expression of worship. Today God does not want us to present Him with dead sacrifices on an altar. Instead He calls us to present ourselves to Him as living sacrifices. Because we have been cleansed by Jesus Christ, God declares us holy and therefore acceptable sacrifices to Him.

An understanding of God's mercy ought to move all believers to worship by giving themselves in total commitment to the Lord. Paul called this presenting of ourselves a "reasonable service." The Greek word translated "reasonable" is the basis for our English word "logical." To give ourselves once and for all to God, in response to His kindness, is logical. We should never fear that once God has control of us He will make our lives miserable. It is illogical to think that God, who has been so merciful in saving us, would suddenly turn unkind to those who worship Him.

True worship is not giving God a percentage of our money, time, and service. True worship is offering yourself to be used by Him at His disposal and for His glory! Have you presented yourself to Him?

BIBLIOGRAPHY

Erdman, Charles R. *The Epistle of Paul to the Romans.* Reprint, Philadelphia: Westminster, 1925.

Gingrich, Roy E. *The Great Theodicy of Paul.* Memphis: Riverside, 1986.

Hendriksen, William. *Romans.* Grand Rapids: Baker, 1980.

Hodge, Charles. *Commentary on the Epistle to the Romans.* 1886. Reprint, Grand Rapids: Eerdmans, 1968.

Lloyd-Jones, D. Martyn. *Romans - The Final Perseverance of the Saints.* Grand Rapids: Zondervan, 1975.

MacArthur, John, Jr. *Security in the Spirit.* Panorama City, CA: Word of Grace, 1985.

McClain, Alva J. *The Jewish Problem and Its Divine Solution.* 1944. Reprint, Winona Lake, IN: B. M. H. Books, 1972.

———. *Romans: The Gospel of God's Grace.* Chicago: Moody Press, 1973.

Packer, J. I. *Evangelism and the Sovereignty of God.* Downers Grove, IL: InterVarsity Press, 1961.

Phillips, John. *Exploring Romans.* Chicago: Moody Press, 1969. Reprint, Neptune, NJ: Loizeaux, 1991.

Stifler, James. *The Epistle to the Romans.* Chicago: Moody Press, 1983.

Thomas, W. H. Griffith. *St. Paul's Epistle to the Romans.* Grand Rapids: Eerdmans, 1946.

Thomson, William M. *The Land and the Book.* 1880. Revised edition, Grand Rapids: Baker, 1966.

Wiersbe, Warren W. *William Culbertson, A Man of God.* Chicago: Moody Press, 1974.

Walvoord, John F. and Roy B. Zuck. *The Bible Knowledge Commentary.* New Testament ed. Wheaton, IL: Victor, 1983.

SCRIPTURE INDEX